Profit Optimization using

ADVANCED ANALYTICS

In the Airline and Travel Industry

Futuristic Systems Beyond Revenue Management

Gopal Ranganathan

CEO, QUAD Optima Analytics

ISBN-13: 9781533184849
ISBN-10: 1533184844

Contents

Figures

Boxes

Acknowledgements

It has been a multi-year effort to write this book but the knowledge and concepts have been in development for 2 decades. My sincere thanks to all close associates and professionals who helped shape the ideas and concepts presented in this book. In particular, I wish to thank Mr. Patrick Edmond, industry expert in Europe, Professor Ram Mohan Pendyala of Georgia Tech and Dr. Emre Serpen, industry expert in Europe for their insights and expert advice. Among the industry mentors who shaped my thinking significantly, special thanks to Mr Ben Vinod of Sabre, Ms. Geeta Jain of CWT India, and Mr. Sudheer Raghavan formerly of Jet Airways.

I wish to acknowledge the unwavering support of my wife, and daughters as I have focused on writing this book. Special thanks to my parents and brother for providing the encouragement needed to start and complete this book.

I dedicate this book to the leaders of the airline and travel industry who provide great service to the business and leisure travelers around the year. Hope they achieve consistently high profits going forward and this book helps them in that pursuit.

Gopal Ranganathan

Chicago

One

Introduction – The Future of Commercial Analytics is Here

To manage in the future executives will need an information system integrated with strategy rather than individual tools used largely to record the past.

—PETER DRUCKER

The total profit margin of the global airline industry in 2014 was 2.6 percent as reported by IATA. Among major industries it ranks lowest in terms of delivering profit margins and returns to shareholders. So far, the Big Data wave has not made a dent to this report card. MIT[i] and McKinsey[ii] research shows Data Driven Decisions can deliver an extra 5-6 percent performance for adopters, outperforming their peer groups. How do we see the future from here? CEOs of the Airline industry will take note of these facts and urge their companies to run differently in the future. The future airline uses Big Data, small data, dark data and smart analytics to change this century long profit draught.

This is not a typical book introduction and its done this way to give an appetizer to the reader of what is possible with advanced analytics. We wish to tell the airline management, in a simple way, how to advance their industry and accelerate toward the future. And so we begin with a scenario of the future and contrast it with today's state. We introduce the future boardroom below to show

how it will function and lay out the advanced analytics business case for the modern airline CEO.

1.1 THE FUTURE BOARDROOM—RUN SIMPLE AND STAY IN CONTROL

The CEO of a global airline enters the boardroom for the monthly review meeting. She has been busy and has not seen a single spreadsheet or PowerPoint in preparation for the meeting. And she is not anxious about it. The executive team too is entering the meeting with similar lack of preparation (the way companies prepare today).

The meeting commences, and the CEO asks the commercial team's Advanced Analytics System (AA System) to display the company forecast against Q2 targets. This system, installed a year back, is the management's operating system. It is available across the network in all the meeting rooms, computers and mobile devices. It uses advanced robotics and machine learning methods in forecasting every performance result and revenue opportunity across the network and keeps the entire commercial team fully informed always. It is able to do this through multidimensional predictive and optimization analytics. The executives responsible for sales channels, regions, customer segments, corporate clients, brand management, route networks and revenue management (RM) use the same system to identify forecast of performance and ways to optimize. The system further presents this information in the same simple and insightful way to everyone from the executives to the frontline staff.

The AA System presents the graph shown in Figure 1. It is rather simple to understand. It is like an Olympic one-hundred-meter racetrack showing the race in lanes. There are six lanes showing the runners (business units) at different points. The CEO sees that the North America business unit is leading at 98 percent. The lane at the bottom represents the race as a whole (a weighted average of all the lanes' achievements), showing the combined forecast for the company at 84 percent achievement to target as of now. Targets and achievement are profit numbers as we will elaborate later.

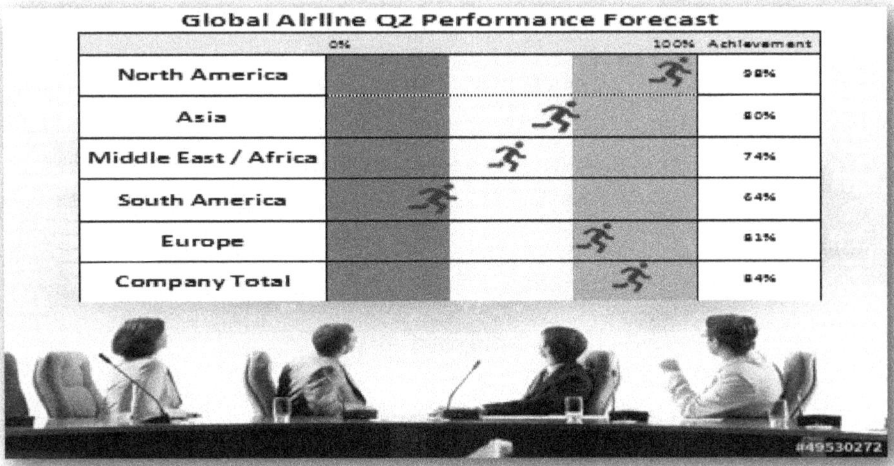
Global Airline Q2 Performance Forecast
0%
100%
Achievement
North America
98%
Asia
80%
Middle East / Africa
74%
South America
64%
Europe
81%
Company Total
84%
#49530272

Figure 1: Future Board at work - using an advanced analytics system

The CEO looks at the head of South America commercial operations which is last in the performance race. She asks for his opinion and plan to improve the result. He taps the screen, asking the system to show the performance drivers in his domain. The AA system presents another graph with lanes and positions of runners in the lanes as shown in Figure 2.

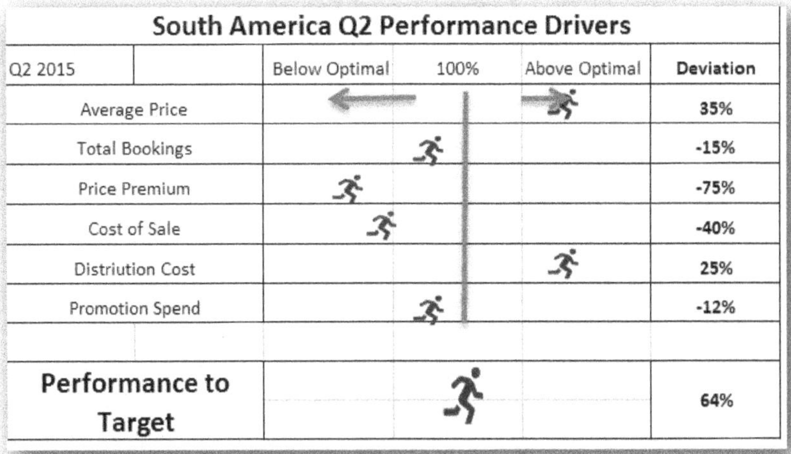
South America Q2 Performance Drivers
Q2 2015
Below Optimal
100%
Above Optimal
Deviation
Average Price
35%
Total Bookings
-15%
Price Premium
-75%
Cost of Sale
-40%
Distriution Cost
25%
Promotion Spend
-12%
Performance to Target
64%

Figure 2: Driver graphs from an advanced analytics system

This is an interesting graph. It shows the forecast of drivers for the quarter and how they can be optimized. The line at the center of this graph represents the optimal values. Any place to the left or right of the line represents a deviation from the optimum. Runners (performance drivers) are spread out uniformly around the center line on the different lanes. The lane at the bottom of the graph shows the performance forecast of the South America operations at 64 percent.

Needing to respond to the CEO's request, he taps the screen again and asks the AA system to optimize his drivers and results. The system updates the graph, moving the drivers to their optimal values while increasing the forecast of South America to 82 percent. This is predictive analytics and optimization at work. The AA system can, on the fly, calculate optimized drivers and results and present that to users.

The CEO is appreciative. She nods and moves on to continue the meeting from there. She asks for each of the region heads to optimize the forecasts. They ask the system to do so. All the other heads of functions also optimize their drivers and the system optimal is a combined 87%, a 3% improvement from current forecast. This is the additional profit margin improvement possible by optimizing drivers using advanced analytics. The entire executive team is on the same page. They can quiz the same system to see the drivers of their specific domains in the optimal scenario.

The board meeting is using a futuristic advanced analytics system that delivers a single version of insights, a term we'd like to coin if it is not already used. We believe it's more useful than the term single version of the truth, which has been around for many years without transformational results. Insights are what the end point of all that data are trying to tell the users and what they need to act. If everyone has the same insights, it makes for a unified executive team, and delivers perfect execution.

1.1.1 THE FUTURE MANAGEMENT TEAM - RUN SIMPLE AND STAY IN CONTROL

The executive management team that attended the CEO's board meeting is dispersed, and each member is now in their domain, driving the best results for the company. The heads of RM, sales, marketing and network planning are working with their teams, driving to 87 percent close for the quarter. In their team meetings, the scenes are the same as at the board meeting: no one is preparing for meetings with excel or PowerPoint reports, yet they are running simple and staying in control.

They have weekly and monthly meetings as preparation and follow-ups to the board meeting. The RM head is chairing his meeting. He starts the meeting the same way by entering the advanced analytics system. He asks the system to display where his department is on Q2 targets as of now (halfway through the quarter) and gets a graph showing him what he wants to know. The RM head sees graphs of regions, routes, and flights, which are in lanes running the race to get to the targets.

We will now present how easily the AA system allows for zooming in and out, providing insights for the right context. The RM head decides he would like to see which flights in Region 2 are doing well and which ones poorly. He taps the system and asks it to display the graph for Region 2 by flights. The system produces the driver graphs for each flight, which show in lanes how each driver is positioned against the optimal value line, which goes down the center of the graph. He then taps the system to optimize the drivers and show him his "plan." The system optimizes drivers of his flights and presents him the graphs. He can accept and implement or he can play around with the drivers and carry out some "what if" analytics. Then he can settle on the drivers that satisfy him will give the best results. That is his plan. He is running simple and is in control.

The above scenarios are played out repeatedly in every executive meeting, every VP's meeting and every manager's meeting. They show the performance forecast for channels, regions, flights, routes, segments, weeks, promotions, salespersons and RM managers. They further drill down to what is causing performance to be off targets and how to move the drivers to optimize the results.

Single version of insights allows management to quickly identify domains that are off target and optimize them. The whole commercial department is in sync and talking from the same page of insights. This is advanced analytics at work.

No one in the team is modeling any of this. The Advanced Analytics system is continuously computing it and showing it in dashboards. Meetings, reviews and discussions flow easily with the aid of the system.

1.2   THE CURRENT STATE OF AIRLINE ANALYTICS

After the US airline industry was deregulated in 1978, there has been a steady increase in interest for quantitative management science. It started with the introduction of "yield management" systems that took the practice of pricing function to a different level not seen before as described in Box 1. This brought about a wave of internal and third-party applications for the commercial and operations areas of airlines. Today yield management has given way to "revenue management," where airlines are focused more on total revenues than on price per booking or yield. Today most modern airlines have a central revenue management department, which drives a significant part of the quantitative agenda that started soon after 1978.

In 1968 American Airlines launched the SABRE computerized reservation system that linked all of the reservation agents around the country. By 1968, American launched its first version (that has since been refined several times) of an automated overbooking process. Without overbooking, American estimates that 15% of the seats on sold out flights would be unused. This overbooking process was the first element in developing a yield management system. Managing ticket sales increased in complexity when American introduced super saver discount fares in 1977 and when the airline industry's schedules and fare structure were deregulated in 1979. With these changes American Airlines moved to develop a yield management system with the goal of "selling the right seat to the right customer at the right time."

De-regulation of the airline industry triggered a major restructuring of flight schedules that further complicated seat allocation. Under de-regulation the airlines moved to develop a hub and spoke system that often had passengers flying into a hub on their way to their final destination. As a result, the yield management system must take into account that some seats on flights between cities must be reserved for connecting flights. An important building block is the forecasting model that estimates demand and cancellation rates. The complexity of the problem eventually led to the development in 1988 of an automated system for yield management, DINAMO. The system's net impact was estimated be $1.4 billion in additional revenues over a three-year period. It also increased the productivity per analyst by 30%. Lastly, the system enabled American Airlines to evaluate the potential of Ultimate Super Saver fares that were priced so low that they could stimulate additional traffic.

Source: "Yield Management at American Airlines", Interfaces, Feb, 1992; hsor.org

Box 1 : American airlines introduced Yield Management in the 1980s

Early adopters of RM techniques had a significant competitive advantage through the 1980s and 1990s. They benefitted from a disciplined approach to segmentation, pricing and inventory management. But since then we have seen increasing numbers of their competitors deploy RM systems, eroding competitive advantage. As this wave driven by RM begins to flatten, most airlines do not see incremental profits being generated by RM techniques alone.

Commercial decision making today goes far beyond automated pricing. It should be optimized all around in the sales, marketing, network planning and RM process. The commercial systems today – including the central RM system – are more "operational" than "analytical" systems. While they allow the commercial functions to carry out the daily tasks of execution, they are not made for supporting enterprise-wide decision-making. As a result, most of the decision making in today's commercial functions is done through the use of excel spreadsheets and PowerPoints. There is no flexibility in the reports and tools that allow for free flowing and fully substantiated meetings leading to the right decisions. We observe that most meetings end with a need for further details and information to enable decision making. Even meetings that arrive at decisions do so, for the most part, with suspect data and models supporting those decisions. Therefore, today's reality of operational systems, excels and PowerPoints in decision making is resulting in a high frequency of poor quality decisions and low profitability of the industry.

Some leading airlines have already started creating advanced analytical systems to help guide them to better margins. But for the majority of airlines that have not yet adopted advanced analytics decision support systems, consistent profit margins are elusive. They will record better margins when overall macroeconomic environment is conducive and falling margins when it is not conducive.

1.3 WHY THIS BOOK?

We (at QUAD Optima Analytics) want to help the airline and travel industry deliver 10-20% more profits. It's possible with advanced analytics (without any further capital infusion and with just better decisions). That is why we wrote this book. We are consultants who have been working with airline and travel industry commercial management for many years. We have seen the change ushered by advanced analytics across other industries. We have been waiting for the airline and travel industry to embrace these opportunities for a data-driven analytics approach to growth and profitability. The opportunity has been promising for the past five years, yet very few companies in this industry have embraced advanced analytics. This book is written with the primary objective of opening up to the commercial leadership the enormous benefits from taking an enterprise approach to advanced analytics. Airlines, hotels, cruise companies, car rental companies, technology companies, and travel agencies all can benefit from this opportunity. We believe they should look at their core capabilities within the functions of RM, sales, distribution and marketing and realize what advanced analytics can do to elevate the execution of the commercial department across these functions.

To be consistently profitable, airlines would need to develop predictive analytics systems at enterprise level. New systems would have to be designed and developed with this DNA in mind. Departmental operational systems, while essential for carrying out their tasks, need to be augmented with cross departmental decision systems driving optimal execution. This is the New Technology wave, as shown in Figure 3. Advanced analytics should enable the best decision-making along this entire process of generating bookings that transcend functional boundaries. Advanced enterprise analytics can drive a dramatic improvement in forecasting, optimization, and profit margins. It is time for the airline industry to embrace and adopt advanced enterprise analytics and improve their profits and returns to shareholders. We hope after reading this book you will be encouraged to jump right into developing an advanced analytics capability for your airline or travel company. If you did that we believe consistent profitability is a very high likelihood in your company's future. This book will explore all the ways to achieving this in greater detail.

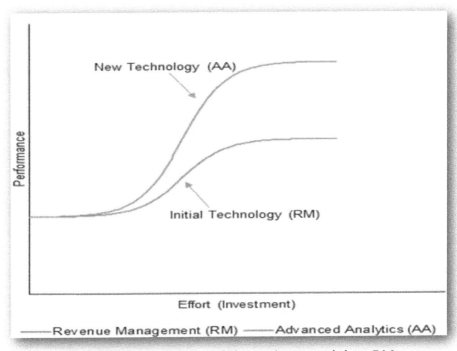

Figure 3: Advanced analytics helps results over and above RM

It is written to make possible the vision shown in section 1.1 and close the gap between that vision and the reality shown in section 1.2. It should greatly benefit anyone making decisions for their company in the airline and travel industry. It is a manifesto for the future board to move to optimization!

1.4   WHAT YOU WILL FIND IN THIS BOOK

We start with showing the imperative for advanced analytics in chapter 2. It lays out the opportunity available to this industry for embracing it at enterprise level over and above RM analytics.

Chapter 3 introduces the reader to the limitations of RM systems of today. It shows how today's capacity based view of demand can be improved with unconstrained demand economics using advanced analytics. It further focuses on limitations caused by inventory control method of pricing and distribution which hamper dynamic pricing and customer lifetime value maximization.

Chapter 4 provides a useful description of Big Data in the airline industry. It shows where significant amount of Big Data exists within airline commercial systems and excel sheets. Tapping into this data is significant for advanced analytics.

Chapter 5 brings out the essence of this book. It lays out what we have seen as the biggest difference between high performing commercial teams and the rest. It describes coordinated commercial execution, starting from focusing on a single metric across the commercial department, to having an integrated advanced analytics system for the commercial team and finally to having a common dashboard.

Chapter 6 describes a modern predictive analytics system stack. It is focused from the CIO perspective and describes how the layered advanced analytics system would come together. It provides a playbook for the CEO to implement the governance process for an advanced analytics capability.

Chapter 7 onwards we focus on execution. This chapter shows the CCO how to develop a modern analytics capability with systems, processes and the talent to drive results. It describes the architecture needed to develop enterprise insights. It then describes the governance process to ensure best results.

Chapter 8 describes the power of dashboard science, which is crucial to delivering the best execution. It lays out the principles of effective dashboards and provides guidance for designing the best commercial dashboards. We introduce gamification based predictive dashboards which are extremely insightful and motivating.

Chapter 9 and 10 provide substantial insights into advanced analytics for the RM and Sales departments. They provide detailed examples in the most critical areas of these functions and show how an enterprise view of these functions is critical for delivering additional revenues over and above their functionally focused results. We show dashboards in action in presenting the insights from the optimization models.

Chapter 11 provides how advanced enterprise analytics are equally applicable to the larger travel industry for delivering incremental results and competitive advantage. We present techniques for the Hotel and Travel Agency industries.

The appendix contains two useful case studies in applying advanced analytics to Sales and RM departments at major airlines. It further presents a paper on multidimensional demand, which is a ground-breaking concept we are bringing forward in this book. We provide a page on a playbook for advanced analytics implementation. Finally, the reader will find a very useful compilation of all the chapter summaries.

In this book we use the words advanced analytics, enterprise analytics and predictive analytics interchangeably. We believe they should all deliver the same great results.

The author has founded a company, Quad Optima Analytics, dedicated to advancing analytics in the airline and travel industry. You can find more at the website www.quadoptima.com on the products and services which are based on the concepts described in this book.

Enjoy!

Two

The Advanced Analytics
Imperative for Airlines

I think historically, the airline business has not been run as a real business. That is, a business designed to achieve a return on capital that is then passed on to shareholders. It has historically been run as an extremely elaborate version of a model railroad, that is, one in which you try to make enough money to buy more equipment.

—*Michael Levine, Executive VP, Northwest Airlines*

A mong major industries, the Airline industry figures lowest in terms of delivering profit margins and returns to shareholders. Figure 4 shows a comparison of US industries and their average profit margins, based on publicly available research from New York University.

Airlines have historically not delivered a good profit margin and return to shareholders. There are pockets in business cycles when airlines show healthy returns, but these are not sustainable over time. Despite consistently good efforts from within the airlines and from partners in the ecosystem, the profit margins continue to be the lowest among all industries.

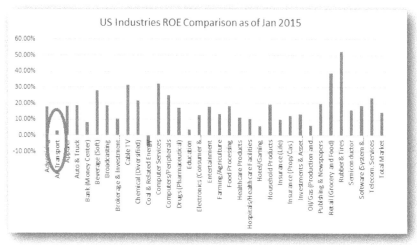

Figure 4: Returns of Airline industry vs other industries

(Source – New York University, Damodaran)

Changing macroeconomic situations may alter the trend to some extent (as the airline industry is one of the most cyclical industries) but will not fundamentally shift the position of the industry with respect to other industries in attracting shareholders and their investments. So this is the imperative for the CEOs and leaders of the major airlines around the world. They would have to find an inflection point and fundamentally alter the game toward higher profits. The advent of Big Data analytics can be seen as an inflection point in the continuum of the airline industry's evolution. We believe it can have a profound impact on long-term profitability and can indeed shift the profit curve upward.

2.1   ADVANCED ANALYTICS—THE OPPORTUNITY FOR THE AIRLINE AND TRAVEL INDUSTRY

We have seen advanced analytics waves hitting us each year in the last five to six years. Many industries have taken to these waves and transformed their economics and performance. Companies within the finance, retail, and Internet industries have been leading the way and reaping rich rewards of profitable transformation.

According to an Amadeus research project by Babson College professor Tom Davenport[iii], the airline industry is behind other industries by several years when it comes to adopting advanced analytics. It is now the opportunity for the airline/ hotel and larger travel industry to invest and find their path to transformation using advanced analytics.

What benefits could airlines get by adopting advanced analytics? Quite simply it would be transformational. We only need to look at the capabilities of industries listed above to know how airlines could benefit. Every aspect of marketing, finance, sales, and customer service would be improved by a step function. The CEO and her team would understand how to win against competition, grow share, and deliver higher profits. Do we say all companies in the other industries have that advantage? No, but these advantages are definitely seen in the companies who adopt and use advanced analytics the right way. On the whole, many industries have a higher number and share of adopters of advanced analytics than the airline industry, and that is the key point to note and compare.

As the book introduction lays out, the imperative is about moving toward the future—running a simple and effective organization that produces results. Better insights land at the fingertips (literally if we use smart phones to deliver the insights) of the CEO, her execution team, the divisional heads, the department heads, the managers, and the frontline analysts. Every manager benefits from having advanced analytics that provide insights into forecast of performance and drivers leading to optimization. If we add in the critical assumption that everyone can be on the same page about the insights, then we are close to the holy grail of management decision-making. The airline of the future can become that today by using advanced analytics and transforming itself.

In airlines of today, we almost invariably find that Big Data analytics is not championed by the business, it is more often championed by the IT department. It typically starts out as projects by departments with the help of the IT department. We believe that today there is no greater imperative for the airline CEO than championing advanced analytics and accelerating this future. That is the easiest way to reach optimization of execution, and there is nothing of greater urgency that the CEO needs to address. Once this shift happens, there will be broad governance driven by the CEO and the C-Suite. That is the best way to deliver on the promise and potential of Big Data advanced analytics.

2.2   THE CEO'S ROLE IN DRIVING ENTERPRISE ANALYTICS

The CEO and her leadership team drive the performance of the airline—commercial and operational—which translates into returns for the shareholder. The primary role for the CEO and management team, then, is to drive higher and higher profit margins, keeping the long-term view while doing so. This further means knowing and shaping the trends that will lead to the most profitable long-term decisions.

Since the advent of Big Data analytics around 2005, the pursuit of better performance through use of analytics has continued to be largely a departmental play. Even in airlines and hotels, analytics has largely been pursued within departments. Furthermore, it is pursued by departmental business leaders in collaboration with IT and data scientists. This practice, while yielding some benefits, does not drive the highest level of insights and cross departmental gains. By not elevating advanced analytics to the level of the CEO and the C-Suite directly, we believe a significant opportunity is lost.

So what does the CEO do to push the case of advanced analytics forward in the organization? In Figure 5 we present the way the C-Suite can begin to drive advanced analytics that permeate the entire organization.

It starts with the realization that just about everything the commercial function does can be driven to a step function improvement through analytics. The CEO with this realization, directs her team to adopt advanced analytics in their domain, while ensuring its governance.

The CFO drives financial analytics at the enterprise level. She is focused on income statement and balance sheet metrics. She champions predictive analytics that forecast and optimize cash flows, revenues, margins, gross operating profits, and investments in the assets of the company. Analytics that show where and how there are increasing opportunities for cash flow and asset creation that increase future cash flows are the focus of financial analytics.

The COO drives operational analytics at the enterprise level. His focus will be metrics like schedule efficiency, on-time departures and arrivals, customer service, baggage handling, safety, and fuel efficiency. Operational analytics are critical for customer satisfaction, brand building, and cost efficiency.

The CIO drives technology adoption that delivers analytics capabilities to all the other departments. She drives metrics like ROI on technology investments, uptime on mission-critical applications, SLAs on various departments' needs, and project metrics for ongoing projects.

The CCO drives the revenue and commercial margin metrics at the enterprise level. Critical metrics tracked by the CCO include sales, revenues, yield, load factors, cost of sale, and cost of distribution. The marketing functions report into the CCO, and they include sales, marketing, revenue management, and network planning. Advanced analytics supporting the CCO at the enterprise level are the focus of this book.

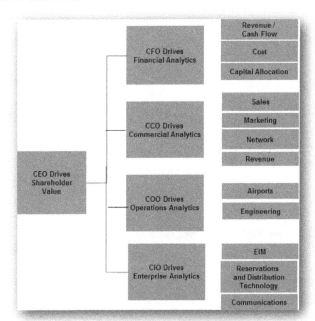

Figure 5: Core analytics supporting
the CEO agenda

We have discussed the main functional areas that the C-Suite is overseeing and the analytics that are powering these areas. We are focused on commercial analytics in this book, but this is one area of the book where we extend the concept of advanced analytics to all the areas being covered by the CEO.

2.3 ADVANCED ANALYTICS—THE CEO'S SOURCE OF COMPETITIVE ADVANTAGE

In the fiercely competitive airline industry, competitive advantage matters a lot. Airlines compete for market share, and in the pursuit of securing higher revenues through higher market share, they incur significant expenses. CEOs and their management teams are constantly looking for the competitive advantage to gain profitable market share. Significant time and effort are spent on formulating strategies that give them even a slight competitive advantage to deliver profits and shareholder value. Advanced analytics offers a significant source of competitive advantage hitherto not recognized or tapped.

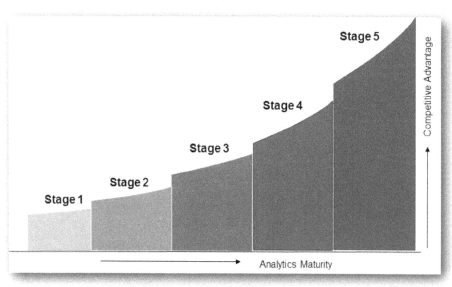

Figure 6: Competitive advantage of analytics innovators

The source of competitive advantage is the difference in maturity levels in adopting and using advanced analytics. Figure 6 illustrates the concept of analytics maturity models and the stages in the maturity process. Innovators are those who have gone past stage 1 and are now in the later stages and realizing significant competitive advantage from adopting an advanced analytics program.

In their book *Analytics at Work*, authors Tom Davenport and Jeanne Harris[iv] further the concept of analytics maturity, which they classify in five stages ranging from stage 1 Analytically Impaired, stage 2 Localized Analytics, stage 3 Analytical Aspirations, stage 4 Analytical Companies to stage 5 Analytical Competitors. They point to the advantages of moving from each stage to the next. These advantages would translate into competitive advantage and shareholder value creation. Underlying the stages of analytics are the type of analytics practiced. These have evolved over time starting from basic information reporting to advanced analytics. We summarize these below.

Analytics 1.0

Stage 1 and 2 airlines are still at Analytics 1.0 and probably use it primarily to have descriptive analytics. In this level of relatively basic expertise, companies are basically able to produce reports that show them how they have done historically. Organizational silos exist, and they see myriad reports, and often a single version of the truth is elusive. These airlines are not able to have good analytics that focus on the future and predict how the drivers are shaping results in the coming months.

Analytics 2.0

Stage 3 and 4 airlines are slightly ahead and have Analytics 2.0 capabilities in place for the most part. They are able to have a good handle on descriptive reports and are also good at looking forward with predictive analytics in place. Organizational silos still exist, and departmental reports still drive most of the decisions. While they are able to have great historical reports and good forward-looking reports in reasonable time, they are, like most airlines, still not able to arrive at a single version of the truth.

Analytics 3.0

Stage 5 airlines are truly ahead of the pack and have Analytics 3.0 capabilities in place. They have a good mastery of descriptive reports and predictive analytics in place at enterprise levels. Most of the airlines are not close to having Analytics 3.0 capabilities and are also not able to arrive at the single version of insights.

So the journey continues, and airlines are striving to get advanced analytics in place, where perfect insights will lead to perfect strategies being executed flawlessly. Box 2 showcases Kayak, one of the best examples of advanced analytics use case in the travel industry. While they are not an airline or even a travel agent, Kayak has played an important role in bringing analytics to the end user in their buying process. In the remaining chapters of this book, we provide a blueprint of how airlines can make progress in this journey.

Kayak: Advanced Analytics Practitioner

Kayak is a high-end user of Big Data technologies, employing them for internal decisions as well as for customer offerings—as most stage 5 practitioners do. In fact, according to their CIO, Kayak is as much a technology company as a travel search provider. About 70 percent of their employees are technology people, with a heavy emphasis on data scientists. Many have advanced degrees. They use predictive analytics to help users with pricing information and the best timing to get the best prices. The predictive analytics also communicate the accuracy and probability of the results. To deliver this to the customers, they use Big Data from various sources including the historical prices, analyses of repeatable patterns, and monitoring of changing current demand. Machine learning algorithms working on Big Data technologies. They present these insights in simple user interfaces that are easy to comprehend, in every format and on every type of device users want, including traditional PCs, tablets, and mobile phones. Most airlines are not at this level of using Big Data to maximize their internal operations and customer value.

Source: https://www.cxotalk.com/data-machine-learning-user-experience-giorgos-zacharia-cto-kayak

---

Box 2: Kayak - a stage 4 advanced analytics practitioner

2.4   ADVANCED ANALYTICS USE CASE EXAMPLES

It is a common perception across industries that advanced analytics entail esoteric models working on parts of the business that cannot be measured easily. Another common perception is that Big Data and advanced analytics are primarily under the purview of IT, and mainstream business does not have much to do with it. Yet another view is that analytics is just old wine in a new bottle—companies have been doing analytics for decades, so this cannot be anything new. And there are many more misunderstandings and misconceptions about the importance and quantification of advanced analytics in driving enterprise profits and shareholder value.

The impact of advanced analytics can be big if leadership recognizes the opportunity and drives a systematic, enterprise-wide program to deliver the benefits. Based on our experiences of running custom enterprise analytics projects, we see it raising top-line revenues by greater than 5 percent and bottom-line improvement of greater than 10 percent. In the rest of this chapter, we will show, through use cases, how such projects can be put together to drive value.

We would like to provide real-life case studies of advanced analytics projects at a few different airlines to set up this discussion of exactly why advanced analytics are needed by the modern airlines.

2.4.1 EXAMPLE 1: ADVANCED ANALYTICS FOR RM AT A REGIONAL FULL-SERVICE AIRLINE

We demonstrate the need and importance of advanced analytics through this example. We were commissioned to improve wholesale the RM analytics at a top regional airline. Appendix 11.2 summarizes the project and the results.

The airline was a top-notch regional full-service carrier with an excellent product, route network, and service. It had been in existence for several years and had a very good brand that was well recognized in its markets. All the key capabilities were in place—RM, sales, network planning, marketing and e-commerce functions were well developed. A world-class reservation system was in place. Alliance and Codeshare partners were in place, and Interlining was in place. Annual traffic growth in that market was around 10 percent, and the airline was experiencing around 15 percent annual growth. But costs were growing equally high, so profitability was elusive.

The RM system in place had already delivered a revenue uplift of 5–10 percent from pre-RM days. So the complex job of lifting revenues by an additional 5 percent was a daunting one. Advanced

RM analytics were employed to get the job done. These were beyond what was possible through the existing RM systems and processes.

Management had not embarked on a change in strategy. The full-service model would continue, and the cost structure would not be changed significantly in any way. The task was very clear: we needed to improve revenue production above the current levels by 5–10 percent without changing the cost structure (i.e., no CASK reduction, but a 5–10 percent RASK improvement).

The RM advanced analytics project focused on drivers of profits using Big Data and advanced modeling for forecasting and optimization. The project produced immediate and lasting results that raised revenues by 5 percent and profit margins by 10 percent. So how was this achieved?

RM systems were not capturing the data needed on the drivers. We ran a series of projects to fix that. For example, the first project was in improving forecast accuracy. We describe some details of how we improved forecast accuracy. RM systems do not provide for continuous monitoring and calibration of forecast accuracy. They are not self-learning systems with feedback and forecast improvement. Instead our observation is that most RM systems need extensive intervention from outside the system to "clean" the data. Even if the data is cleaned, these systems do not have built-in mechanisms to improve the forecast by learning from past forecasts. This has to be done by using external analytics and then manually fine-tuning the forecasting system by calibrating the parameters correctly. Beyond forecasting, we focused on several other projects. RM systems were not identifying down-selling by sales teams across the networks, leading to pricing inversion. They were not spotting sales slowdowns on weak flights well in advance to enable correction. The leg segment based RM system was incapable of handling poor connecting traffic forecast and yield drops. All this was corrected using advanced analytics outside of RM systems.

We will be returning to this example of RM analytics in the later chapters to throw light on all the aspects of the projects. At this point we want to highlight that it is possible to drive the additional revenues out of RM and other systems simply by driving advanced analytics and improving the performance of these systems.

2.4.2 EXAMPLE 2: ADVANCED ANALYTICS FOR SALES AT A GLOBAL AIRLINE COMPANY

Next we turn to an example of advanced analytics based sales transformation at a large global airline. The global airline had a large worldwide network and had not been consistently profitable. It had both large international and domestic networks. Revenues were rather flat over many years, costs were steadily increasing above the revenue levels, and many quarters saw the airline reporting operating and financial losses. The airline had quite sophisticated RM systems and a large IT department that supported a robust IT system.

> Sales at this global giant was underperforming. It was not functioning with the smartness that the stature of the airline would demand. The project was commissioned to integrate and deliver an analytics standard that would lift the execution of the sales force by an order of magnitude. This was the mission of the sales transformation analytics effort.

Management commissioned a large program to transform sales execution and drive better commercial performance. As part of the project, we delivered an advanced analytics capability to the sales department. Before the transformation project began, the sales department did not have standardized data sources and repositories to carry out analytics on a regular and repeatable basis. As part of the transformation project, we built a significant data management capability through which advanced analytics could be run daily and continuously. This is one of the themes we highlight throughout the book—analytics should be driving the business daily and continuously, not just when transformational projects are commissioned.

Appendix 11.3 summarizes the project and shows the different modules executed during the sales transformation program. It was comprehensive, ranging from sales structure, to customer segmentation, pipeline improvement, contract modeling and cost reduction. The aim for the set of projects was to provide a step-function change in the capability of the sales force and revenue growth while not adding to cost. It was largely achieved as shown in the results tabulated against each project as well as in the overall project summary at the bottom of the table. In addition to the immediate quantification of improved revenues, the project lifted the capability of the airline's sales department. It allowed for embedding advanced analytics into daily execution of the sales function from leadership down to managers.

Driving a sustainable 15 percent revenue growth at a large global airline is nearly impossible without something as powerful as embedded advanced analytics. We will return to this example many times in the book to underscore the core concepts of how advanced analytics would improve core execution.

2.5 TAKEAWAYS

- Profitability of the airline industry is the lowest compared to most other industries.
- The vast majority of airlines do not have consistent profits across business cycles.
- Analytics innovation has not taken place in the airline industry as it has in other leading industries.
- Revenue management analytics has not progressed beyond its original and limited (in today's Big Data environment) paradigms of forecasting and optimization.
- Advanced analytics must be adopted by the airline industry to make it more profitable over the next few decades and restore competitiveness with other industries in turning profits.
- The CEO is the main executive who should "get this" and exhort her leaders to adopt and deliver advanced analytics. She should drive the governance of advanced analytics deployment and be on top of the review of results
- Competing airlines range from stage 1 to stage 5 in using analytics. Those in stage 5 would have a significant competitive advantage leading to increased profitable market share. They are practicing descriptive, prescriptive and predictive analytics.
- Advanced analytics uses cases of RM and Sales analytics at client airlines reveals the scope of improvements can range from 5% to 15% revenue improvements.

Three

Revenue Management
Oriented Analytics of Today

Revenue Management is selling the right seat to the right customer at
the right price at the right time

—*Common Definition of RM*

Since the advent of "yield management" at American Airlines in the early
1980s, the practice of analytics within most airlines is centered on the RM
department. The commercial agenda is centered on annual revenue planning
driven by the CCO in close cooperation with the RM head. While sales, marketing and network planning departments are critical in execution, it is the
information stored within the RM systems—bookings, yields, revenues both
historical and forward —that are the heartbeat of the modern airline analytics.
It is very RM-centric. It is as good as the RM systems allow it to be. As good
as they have been to delivering great results in the past 30 years, we observe
several limitations in today's RM systems that are holding airlines back from
enterprise optimization. Modern airlines need to move out of RM centricity
and into the realm of enterprise analytics to overcome these limitations.

3.1   WHY IS ANALYTICS IN AIRLINES RM-CENTRIC TODAY?

Revenue is planned and measured along routes in most airlines today. RM is the
one department that has full end-to-end view of routes. They have the systems

and the staff to monitor and maximize the revenues of the routes. Execution is across all departments, but measurement is usually along routes by RM function. This is the basis for the commercial department's analytics today. It is very RM centric and is holding back other functions from being strong analytics players and driving performance higher.

3.1.1   THE REVENUE MANAGEMENT SYSTEMS IN AIRLINES TODAY

RM systems date back to the 1980s, when data modeling was in its infancy and the databases used to store the data were not evolved to how we see them today. These systems were built in keeping with databases and computing constraints of the day. Today we have come a long way in terms of these constraints, yet the RM system modeling has not changed in any fundamental way. They follow the same basic building blocks for inventory-based pricing controls as shown in Figure 7.

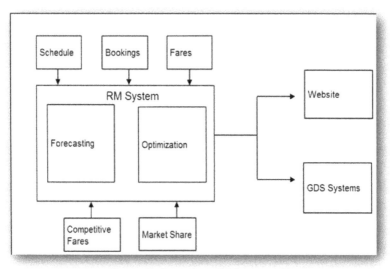

Figure 7: A modern RM system

The core of RM systems are the forecasting and optimization modules. They take inputs from historical bookings (demand), current schedule (capacity) and fares (market conditions). Competitive fares are used as inputs into some RM systems, but they don't impact forecasting or optimization in most systems. Additionally, in some RM systems, market share data may be fed into the system, primarily to enable end users to make informed decisions, not for modeling. This has been the basic architecture of the modern RM system for twenty years now. There have been very few changes in inputs or outputs or the core mathematical modeling within the system. In the following paragraphs these inputs are discussed in greater detail.

Bookings inputs are the core data on which the RM system operates. Bookings are usually available from a Passenger Name Record (PNR) database within the reservations system, which feeds the RM system. RM systems can either be fed directly from a source system or from an offline source. Historical demand and remaining demand sourced from bookings data at flight booking class level are the central measures within an RM system.

Schedules inputs are used to calculate remaining capacity for each iteration of the forecast and optimization. Many airlines do not feed daily schedule changes into the RM system. Schedule inputs to the RM system may not exactly reflect the deployed network. This could result in errors in forecasting and optimization that could be large depending on the percentage deviation.

As RM systems and route networks evolved, the complexity of fare inputs steadily increased. Some airlines have managed to address this, but the vast majority of airlines—which includes most LCCs in the world—run the simplest RM systems fed by basic fare inputs. In Leg-Segment RM systems, the fare inputs are at leg booking class level (a leg is non-stop flight). In Origin and Destination (O&D) RM systems, the fare inputs are at O&D level, which is how bookings are sold. Even today most airlines run Leg-Segment RM. While the product sold may be across connecting flights, fares and inventory control in these systems are at leg (or single flight) level. This causes a significant issue in pricing complex products that go beyond the single leg. It calls for fare construction and publishing capability that far exceeds the sophistication of the airline. It becomes a bottleneck in the support structure for evolving business models. The reality is that many airlines that were once point-to-point airlines have started feeding connecting traffic through hubs and partner airlines. Their RM systems still optimize revenues as if they were not connecting traffic through hubs. Advanced analytics can address these limitations and drive more revenue out of the system.

3.1.2   THE EVOLUTION OF REVENUE MANAGEMENT – STRATEGIC PRICING TO TACTICAL DISCOUNTING

Yield Management started with the remarkable strategy by American Airlines[v] to use technology and marketing (in an unprecedented way) to neutralize an emerging LCC with lower fares. Over the years the focus shifted from yield to total revenue maximization. Today's RM departments are concerned with increasing revenues by increasing yield and volumes. Sales and marketing departments are concerned primarily with increasing demand in the marketplace, thereby contributing to volumes and revenues. While they can be both strategic and tactical, RM tends to be primarily tactical. Its very definition is to be tactical. Pricing is a strategic function, but its implementation through the RM function makes it appear to be tactical.

So let's explore where the tactical focus of RM comes from. When the airline industry in the United States was deregulated in 1978 and free market pricing and competition were encouraged, these changes fostered strategic thinking in using the pricing function to gain competitive advantage. Market segmentation and pricing came together in this amazing concept. Suddenly the industry was introduced to a new way of looking at what customers might be willing to pay and what airlines could charge for them. A seat was no longer seen as just a seat. The timing of when that seat was purchased made all the difference to what price an airline could extract from it. This produced great results for American Airlines and soon put competition out of business—the ultimate outcome of a successful strategy. Moreover, what started as a strategy produced great repeatable results that could be codified in systems thinking. That was the beginning of RM systems.

The RM system was developed by business working closely with the IT department within an airline. Once the results were evident, there was a need to have such systems at many airlines, and soon a market developed for this type of system. In fact, before the 1980s, RM as a department did not exist. Not only did this create a new type of system that airlines did not previously have, but it also defined new processes within airlines' commercial departments. The modern RM department was born and with it a new way of merchandizing and distributing airline supply.

As RM evolved, it needed people, process, and technology to support the function. Large airlines set up sophisticated departments housing hundreds of analysts. In most airlines two separate departments were set up—pricing and inventory control. Pricing departments were responsible for defining the product price and the various fare classes associated with product definition. Inventory control departments—commonly called RM departments—were concerned with using the RM system to set limits on seats to be sold at each fare level. Thus the twin functions of pricing and inventory control were set up at most airlines over the past three decades.

This process was put in place in large airlines to start with, but over the years it has become common among most of the airlines in the world. Today both FSC and LCC carriers have started using RM systems and RM teams to maximize revenues. This has led to a situation where RM is a core process among most of the airlines. Over the years the competitive advantage from having and using RM systems and process has been blunted as almost all the competitors have these systems.

Customers have grown accustomed to RM pricing mechanisms. They have been trained into understanding where and how to get the best deals to lower their total cost of travel year-round. This has further blunted the ability of RM techniques to deliver competitive advantage and incremental revenues.

3.2   ECONOMICS OF REVENUE MANAGEMENT

RM is essentially a pricing process, but the RM systems commercially available today are not pricing systems. They are inventory control systems. This is one of the most limiting aspects of today's airline pricing process preventing it from being nimble and effective. In fact, most airlines that have an RM system also need a pricing system to do the pricing functions. So what exactly does an RM system do? In this section we will take a deep dive into the economics of pricing and explain in those terms how today's modern RM systems function.

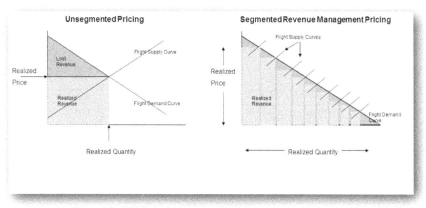

Figure 8: RM systems introduced segmented pricing

Market pricing is based on simple economics of demand and supply. But airline pricing as an economics science application got real only after deregulation of the US airline industry in 1978. Figure 8 shows airline pricing economics before and after deregulation. The left panel shows the pre-deregulation pricing science and the right panel shows the post deregulation pricing science. On the left is basically unsegmented pricing, where the price is more or less fixed for the entire flight based on one price value. There is no understanding of customer segments, their differing willingness to pay, and the pricing reflecting this difference and maximizing revenue. Post deregulation, airlines had an opportunity to set prices according to market principles, without government intervention to protect particular segments of airlines, but focused more on providing the best economics for customers. Some airlines like pioneer American Airlines recognized this opportunity and set in motion strategies that became incorporated as pricing strategies of revenue management (then called yield management). This was based on the principles of customer segmentation and understanding the airlines' abilities to set and extract different prices from different customer segments. The right panel shows the segmentation approach started by RM. As we can see in the conceptual explanation in these figures, the realized revenue is very high and nearly maximized, because consumer surplus is reduced compared to the panel on the left. This represented a significant technology improvement, with fantastic revenue gains. Many early adopters saw gains of 5–10 percent in revenues, most of which went straight to the bottom line because there was little overhead spent to achieve these gains. Yet as we saw more and more airlines adopt RM technology, the gains started slowing by the early 2000s, and today it has been flat for many years.

Continuing with discussing the right panel of Figure 8, we see how RM today is achieving revenue maximization. It is focused on customer segmentation as implemented through fare classes. For each fare class, there is a supply curve that works on the single demand curve of the full flight. This produces many intersection points that become the inventory available at each price point. It improves significantly from the unsegmented pricing before revenue management, but leaves it short by 4–5 percent of maximization (per our estimates).

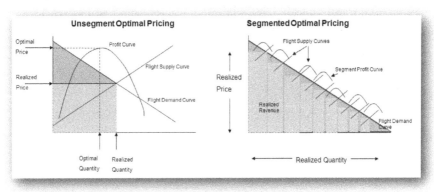

Figure 9: Optimized RM with dynamic pricing

Figure 9 shows how to improve on RM inventory control approach to segmented pricing. It is simple in concept as shown in the left panel. It shows that the peak profit point is not necessarily the same as the realized price (yield). The optimal price to charge for inventory in a booking class changes with demand and supply dynamically. RM's booking class approach to setting inventory in a class at the same price is sub-optimal. The right approach would be to identify the demand equation and set prices for each booking class as a dynamic point. The Bid Price approach to RM pricing achieves this in a limited way. Bid Price is usually calculated by RM systems as the slope of the revenue function at a given leg capacity[vi]. While it is certainly better than the static pricing of booking class inventory, it is still a capacity led pricing approach than market demand led pricing. Further, Bid Price calculations are also made with constrained demand economic analyses. Advanced analytics uses dynamic pricing of unconstrained demand (see section 3.3 for further discussion on this).

Using unconstrained demand to improve the economics of revenue management has been a goal of RM departments for many years. But this problem has not been solved as the input systems and data processing methods have changed little. Systems and data notwithstanding, we believe, there has to be a paradigm shift in understanding customer behavior. Transactions shaped by capacity constraints do not describe true customer behavior. Instead the focus should shift in tracing and understanding repeated interactions of the customer entity across time and across other dimensions. This is the core paradigm shift needed in understanding customer behavior.

It starts by understanding the multidimensional space in which demand and supply interact.

Figure 10 shows demand generated across Point of Sale (POS), channels, and segments for various routes. Modern revenue management systems forecast demand at flight-booking class and departure level. As the figure shows Routes or Flights are only one of the dimensions of understanding demand. Customers (frequent fliers or corporate clients or even VFR – visiting friends and relatives - customers) who are booking on one flight are also booking on other flights. Similarly, POS that contribute to one flight also contribute to many other flights. Channels that contribute to one flight also contribute to other flights. Following this logic, we see that optimizing one flight at a time (as today's RM systems do)

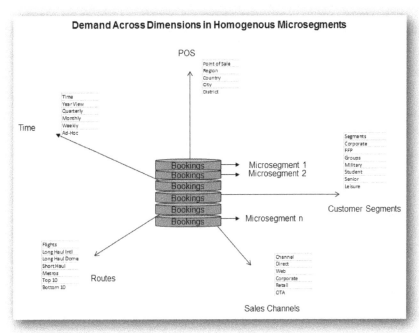

Figure 10: Multidimensional demand in Microsegments

leads to suboptimal results. The right way to understand and model demand is to look for consistent multidimensional demand segments and track their behavior over time.

We believe the new advanced analytics should define microsegments which span dimensions. Figure 10 shows bookings in microsegments that span dimensions. These microsegments track behavior of homogenous bookings and indicate the movement of drivers to vastly improve forecasting and optimization across the revenue network, not just one flight. This type of optimization could improve results by 5% in our estimates based on projects executed (examples in appendix).

3.3   TECHNICAL LIMITATIONS OF TODAY'S RM SYSTEMS

While many other industries have taken advantage of recent advances in Big Data technologies, the airline industry has been a laggard in the field, especially for pricing and commercial functions. With the advent of Big Data computing hardware and software to process massive amounts of data in real time, we now have the right opportunity. Let's start understanding the basics of this innovation by focusing first on the most important piece in driving higher profits for the industry: demand and how to understand and use it to drive profits.

3.3.1   UNIDIMENSIONAL DEMAND FORECASTING DOES NOT SEE THE FULL PICTURE

Accurate demand forecasting is a key driver of airline profits. There are many examples to show that a forecast accuracy improvement of 10 percent can result in revenue improvement of 1 percent[vii]. Today at the lowest level of granularity (flight-booking class level), even the best airlines are not able to achieve a forecast accuracy of 85 percent. Airline demand is shaped by drivers across multiple dimensions beyond just routes and fare class. Examples of dimensions usually ignored by RM demand forecasting include Geography (Point of Sale), Channels, Sales teams, Customer segments among many others. Glossing over these dimensions leads to incorrect mapping of drivers to results and wasted sales and marketing efforts.

3.3.2   CONSTRAINED DEMAND FORECASTING IS NOT ACCURATE

RM systems use bookings to quantify demand. They allocate seats on a given flight to the booking classes. Once the number of seats allocated is sold, the booking class is closed. More bookings looking for seats in that class (at that price and with those fare rules) are not accepted. They cannot track bookings that are denied when the booking class is closed. This was true of the earliest RM systems and its true of today's RM systems. So in essence airlines are always underestimating the "true" demand, which should be unrestricted by capacity or management decisions. The censoring is taking place in the way airlines are choosing to see demand. This is what we call constrained demand forecasting. It can lead to as much as 3 percent revenue loss[viii].

3.3.3   TIME SERIES FORECASTING IS UNRELIABLE AND INACCURATE

Today's RM systems use forecasting techniques that date back twenty years at least. They use historical time series and exponential smoothing techniques on flight-booking class level historical demand. Structural changes in demand drivers over the last twenty years have made this technique quite unreliable as RM systems evolved. We see that most RM systems do not achieve more than 85% forecast accuracy, something airline commercial leaders are not satisfied with. The major structural changes driving this unreliable forecast are:

1. Breakdown of fare rules which are the basic method of inventory control in RM systems, driven by incursion of LCCs.
2. Falling prices driven by transparency of fares in the internet channels

These twin factors have led to traditional fare fences being torn down and demand spiraling down. What was once a reliable technique of using historical demand within these fences has now fallen apart. Along with this the reliability of time series models too has fallen apart.

With the advent of Big Data analytics, we can now track significantly more valuable data on drivers of demand. We are observing more use of regression forecasting techniques, which can produce stunningly accurate demand forecasts even with just a few weeks of historical data. Older methods like time series methods need months and months of historical data to "train" the model.

3.3.4   INVENTORY CONTROL, IS NOT QUITE DYNAMIC PRICING

The focus of RM systems, since the early days, has been on inventory control rather than on dynamic pricing. According to Ben Vinod, an industry leader in RM science, RM has always focused on what the supplier is willing to accept rather than what the customer is willing to pay[ix]. That is, RM is supply-side focused rather than being customer-centric.

This poses a significant problem for customer segmentation if the underlying segments are purely defined by price and if fare rules suddenly mean very little for customers. This is what transpired with the advent of the LCCs and with the increasing role of the Internet channel. Customer segmentation is in disarray at most airlines, and with it inventory control based pricing.

So we have established that inventory control-based RM systems are not able to change the price differentially based on customer profiles and choices. As dynamic pricing is not practiced in reality, pockets of revenue opportunities are left untapped by the current methods of RM in most airlines today.

3.3.5   RM PROCESS IS TRANSACTIONAL, AGNOSTIC TO CUSTOMER LIFETIME VALUE

RM systems are not able to change price differentially based on customer profiles and choices. As a result, customer lifetime values are not factored in directly in evaluating RM pricing or inventory control decisions. In today's RM systems two customers are equal if they pay the same price for the inventory that is available for sale to them. Their historical purchases or future likelihood of purchases do not get factored in. This results in a very short term approach to looking at customers for transaction value maximization (today's RM) and not lifetime value maximization.

3.3.6   RM SYSTEMS ARE NOT BUSINESS INTELLIGENCE SYSTEMS

RM systems are designed to be operational systems with a focus on automated pricing decision support. The optimization programs work on the internal data to optimize inventory control decisions. These decisions are set in the system and shown to the analyst on their workbench. Analysts have the options of accepting these decisions or overriding them with their own recommendations. Apart from this, the RM systems are not designed to produce any meaningful business intelligence interfaces and reports as they are built for operational purposes of automating decision support.

Yet many airlines use RM systems to generate bookings and RASK reports, which are used to make the critical decisions. Some airlines export data from RM systems into enterprise database repositories to produce these reports. Others use reports available in the RM systems. In either type of BI approach, data ends up in standard reports or within Excel spreadsheets. These reports are nothing more than data dumps of historical and future bookings. They are not sophisticated model outputs designed to deliver insights from the raw data. They cannot perform scenario analyses. They are not built to answer the questions that lead to strategic decisions. RM is focused on tactics, so the reports that come out of the RM systems are not designed to answer the big strategic questions.

Leaders in the commercial department need insights on performance and drivers. They leave tactical decisions to the RM systems and RM teams. In meetings they would expect to see reports that show predicted performance, gaps to targets, and drivers of these gaps. Advanced analytics will enable the commercial team to use information from RM systems to deliver those insights.

3.3.7 RM SYSTEMS CANNOT ASSESS IMPACT OF COMMERCIAL ACTIONS

RM systems are driving a lot of conversation around the commercial department as the most advanced analytics systems an airline can expect to have. Yet they are poorly designed to answer even the most basic questions about impact of Commercial actions.

RM systems cannot quantify the impact of any of the 4 Ps of marketing - Price, Promotions, Placement and Product. RM systems do not factor in these critical drivers of demand. So any activity that is driving demand is implicitly captured in the time-series modeling of historical demand.

RM systems cannot quantify the impact of a price change. RM systems may be able to solve complex inventory control using OR techniques and generate bid prices, but they cannot actually tell you how changing the price for the corporate segment (or a corporate entity) may affect the profits of a company. This is a relatively simple analysis that RM systems are not wired to do. Yet it is one of the most basic types of analytical help the commercial department managers need.

RM systems cannot quantify the impact of a marketing or promotional event. It will have to be done in Excel, and that quantification will probably will be wrong. RM systems of today are less aligned with marketing and sales decisions than they are with pricing decisions.

3.4 TAKEAWAYS

- Analytics in airlines today is very centered on the revenue management function. Historically RM has been the main function with full access to all the critical information about flight demand and revenues, which are stored in RM systems.
- The core design and architecture of RM systems has not changed much since the advent of early systems nearly thirty years back. They focus on historical bookings and the characteristics of the bookings to forecast future demand and revenues.
- RM systems were introduced in the 1980s to serve a strategic need to bring competitive advantage using cutting-edge pricing and marketing analytics. But since then, RM has become increasingly tactical in its focus and has lost the strategic edge of dynamic pricing.
- RM economics is based on constrained supply and demand. This results in a systematic bias in forecasting and optimization leading to loss of revenue.
- RM systems are based on inventory control of Fare classes. This system may be in place due to the current GDS distribution systems, but bottom line is that it does not allow for true dynamic pricing. This results in loss of revenue.
- Demand forecasting in today's RM systems is single or two dimensional at best, focusing on routes and flights as one dimension and fare class as another dimension. They cannot forecast demand along other dimensions such as POS, channels, customer segments.
- RM systems are transactional and focus on the best possible yield (or revenue) the system can deliver given capacity and demand. They do not factor in the life time value of customers when deciding on optimal value to charge.
- Today's RM systems have evolved from yield to revenue focus, but have not yet graduated toward margin and value focus. This results

in suboptimal delivery of the main metrics of the commercial department—the highest possible commercial margins.

- Multidimensional unconstrained demand forecasting and optimization using advanced analytics is the next level of enterprise RM.

Four

Big Data Driving Advanced Analytics

Big Data will spell the death of customer segmentation and force the marketer to understand each customer as an individual.

—*Ginni Romnetti, CEO, IBM*

Since 2010, there has been a tectonic shift in the amount of data and computing capability dedicated to analytics. Regular business analysis took a definitive turn toward a new discipline called "Big Data analytics." It has caught the imagination of all companies, the IT and management consulting industry, business schools, and just about everybody else. As early as in a 2011 report, the McKinsey Global Institute[x] said, "Big data will become a key basis of competition, underpinning new waves of productivity growth, innovation and consumer surplus." Indeed, there are numerous such indications, references, and quotes. All this attention has sparked a lot of discussion on the ROI from Big Data analytics. There is very little evidence of the ROI in company annual reports or in literature. This has led to questions about the reality and the hype surrounding Big Data. In this chapter we will give the reader a clear perspective on Big Data in the airline and travel industry. It shows how using it makes possible improved business performance as seen in brand perception, product development, pricing, customer service, and ultimately higher profit margins.

4.1   BIG DATA IN THE AIRLINE INDUSTRY

Big Data is commonly quoted as having three characteristics—volume, variety, and velocity—that make it significantly "bigger" than what we have seen before. That is not exactly a definition of Big Data, but more a definition of what today's data is not. It is not so useful when we consider how this definition helps us build future decision systems. We believe Big Data is definitely that, but also more tangibly, it is attribution and growth of transactional data. Attribution that allows for meaningful drill down from aggregates to details for uncovering the truth.

We begin first with understanding attribution. Attribution is adding details to what is normally found in the transactions. For example, in an airline it could mean details of transactions that are customer interactions captured in the other systems of the company, such as on Facebook pages. If there is a way to link these separate data into the transactions, it adds significant information to the transactions about the customer. Another example can be seen in demographic or financial details of clients. All this is attribution that describes the transactions in richer details.

In the above example, we saw two types of transactions on which Big Data attribution is shown. One is existing transactions (bookings), and the other is new transactions (website visits, Facebook comments, etc.). So what we are commonly calling Big Data is coming in the form of an enormous increase in new transactions (not just bookings) and an enormous increase in attribution (details) of these transactions (bookings and others). This combination is producing a very rich and exploding data capture called Big Data. Similar to the BCG matrix for company strategy, we can present your Big Data strategy by viewing it along the dimensions of growth of transactions and the growth of attribution in the data.

Figure 11 shows in two dimensions and in four quadrants the explosion we are seeing in Big Data. The two dimensions are transactions dimension (x axis) and attribution dimension (y axis). Transactions growth is mainly new information coming in the form of more data records in the company's

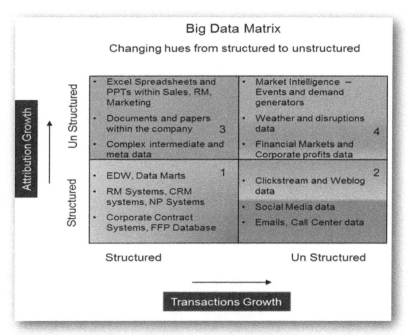

Figure 11: Big Data growth 2 x 2 matrix

systems collected from new sources. Attribution growth is mainly richer information on existing records in the company's systems collected from new and existing sources. The figure further shows emergence of unstructured data as a critical component of Big Data. Growth on both dimensions increasingly is driven by unstructured data. Quadrant 1 is purely structured data within the systems that are formally recognized as data. Quadrant 2 and 3 are increasingly unstructured data that are sitting in systems that are part of the company today, but which are not formally recognized as data. Quadrant 4 is mostly unstructured and not within the company's systems today. This is currently external, but it has a real impact on the company's various decisions.

Most airlines today would be in Quadrant 1, where they understand and want to tap into structured data within their systems. Quadrant 2 and 3 Big Data already exists in various databases and islands of data within these airlines but is not formally recognized and used for advanced analytics.

4.1.1   BIG DATA WITHIN COMMERCIAL SYSTEMS

Quadrant 1 in our Big Data matrix is about structured data found within exist-ing systems used by airlines internally or from external sources. Today's airlines have structured data in several different operational and decision-support envi-ronments. They include:

- RM and pricing systems
- Network planning and scheduling systems
- CRM or SFA systems
- GDS or distribution systems
- CRS or reservation systems, also known as PSS
- External market share data systems such as MIDT, Pax IS, or Sabre's Global Demand Data
- External pricing data feeds such as those from ATPCO and Infare
- Corporate sales agreement systems such as Prism
- External data feeds from agency data systems such as ARC or BSP
- Loyalty program systems
- Enterprise data warehouse and other system-based data and reporting environments

The above list is indicative of the breadth of systems in today's airline commer-cial departments. They hold data within their databases that are not connected and hence are virtual stovepipes of data. There is often overlap between systems and data silos, but that is really pointing to the larger problem rather than any solution.

Let's explore the data in some of these systems.

Example 1—Big Data in silos in RM, loyalty, and sales systems
RM systems have historical bookings data by flight booking class and departure date. They also have bookings for future flights. They use this information to model and predict demand and optimize pricing. While this activity is going on, the loyalty program systems have data that details activities by the airline for

increasing demand within the loyalty base. Similarly, sales systems like Prism have data on activities, contracts, and promotions that the corporate team is driving with corporate clients.

Example 2—Big Data in pricing systems

Pricing systems are used to set strategic and tactical price points. Yet very few pricing systems are able to offer rigorous analyses to back up the pricing decisions. They use internal bookings data to compute price elasticity for the typical pricing analyses. But in the modern Big Data era, basic pricing elasticity analyses using internal historical bookings is inadequate to say the least. For instance, if pricing actions are designed to change market share, Big Data analytics would require a careful and clear understanding in real time of how share is being impacted by pricing. We know that market share and bookings data do not co-exist in any pricing system. This gap should not exist in real-time Big Data systems, which can sense cause and effect in real time in the microsegments, as they house bookings, pricing, and market share data in the same system.

> The RM system is not integrated with the loyalty system and the sales system in real time. Hence the data detailing all the activities in the loyalty and sales systems are not available to the RM system. So demand forecasting, which is a primary feature of the RM system, is agnostic to the activities that are creating the demand as being recorded in the loyalty and sales systems. Attribution of the core transactions within the RM system with Loyalty and Sales data would solve this.

4.1.2   BIG DATA IN EXCEL

Traditional business intelligence (BI) brings information to users from data sources through reports and dashboards. In reality, BI systems serve as a starting point rather than end points in most decision-making processes. Rarely do we see reports leading directly to decision making in senior management context.

Management decisions are mostly made after extensive and laborious modeling work on Excel spreadsheets and translations to PowerPoint presentations. As decision models in Excel become pervasive, executive setups are loaded with teams of experts to drive analytics and BI. Let's look at some examples to show how pervasive the use of Excel is in airline management today. These are typical meetings we see happening at most airlines.

4.1.2.1 *Data within Excel at Sales Leadership Meetings*

The scene is the annual sales leadership meeting of regional managers reporting into the VP of sales. The agenda includes a review of achievement to targets of each leader and plans for coming months and quarters. If the airline has implemented a sales CRM system, such as the one from SalesForce.com, a ready report is available showing sales achievement to targets for each regional leader. Since many airlines do not have such a system, BI systems would produce the reports for them.

The meeting starts with each manager showing their achievement to targets for the past period. As noted, BI systems can help the managers get to this information without too much difficulty. However, when the discussion moves to opportunity and plans for the next quarter, the BI system report is out of its depth. This is where we have observed that standard reports are not available in *any* system for the sales team today showing forecasted achievement to targets. The regional managers would typically produce their own versions of achievement to targets that are presented at the meeting. To do this, they would import data (sometimes lot of it and quite complex data) into Excel spreadsheets, run models and keep reviewing the results till it is ready to present and take decisions. We see Excel making its way into the decisions process because standard sales systems do not have predictive modeling capabilities.

So what is the Big Data in sales leaders' Excel spreadsheets? Bookings, yield, sales, O&D, date, flight, price premium, channel, POS, Cost of Sale (COS), tactical offerings, segment, FFP attributes, booking velocity, client attribution, Quality of Service Indicator (QSI), market Share, capacity Share. Its everyday data for airlines, not some esoteric set of data the managers never see. But if they had a Big Data analytics system, it would tap into this data continuously, feeding analytics that produce insights daily, freeing up the managers to do what they are hired to do. Unfortunately, till such systems are available, Excel and PowerPoint run meetings and import bits and pieces of Big Data on demand creating a governance nightmare for truth. It is wrong and very expensive and something profit seeking airlines cannot afford to do much longer.

4.1.2.2 *Data within Excel at Revenue Management Meetings*

We next look at a revenue management departmental meeting bringing in all RM analysts and flight managers to meet with the VP of RM. The agenda includes a review of achievement to targets of each flight manager and plans for coming months. RM systems can produce data on flight revenues in the past and forecasts of revenues in the future. This allows for each flight manager to prepare these reports for the monthly meeting.

The interesting aspect again is with the follow-up analytics needed when discussing opportunities and risks. This requires predictive modeling and what-if analytics. To answer the questions that may come up in the meetings regarding opportunities and risks, they would import revenue forecast data into their Excel spreadsheets and model it out. So what is the Big Data in their Excel files? Bookings, yield, sales, O&D, date, flight, price premium, channel, POS, COS, tactical offerings, segment, FFP attributes, booking velocity, client attribution, and distributor GDS.

The above data is spread out in various Excel spreadsheets undergoing transformations and modeling to produce insights. Again, like in the sales meetings preparations, there are absolutely no standards guiding the data imported into Excel or for the modeling within the Excels. This is the main problem we see with Big Data in Excel as it does not get treated with the sanitized carefulness that enterprise analytics require.

4.1.3 STREAMING BIG DATA

Today's modern airline has a variety of data sources that are producing streaming (continuously flowing) data in different velocities for the organization to consume. We list a few examples of streaming data seen in airlines:

PNR Data: These are bookings coming in at a tremendous rate in the organization. A regional airline with $1 billion in annual revenues will generate about five thousand PNRs per day. PNRs contain a significant amount of information about the sales of the company, the channels, the customers, the loyalty membership details, corporate deals, and so on. This rapidly streaming data is a gold mine of information that is at the foundation of structured Big Data for an airline. The value of streamed PNR data is significantly increased if it is used to uncover emerging trends along various dimensions such as customer segments, channels, and booking regions. PNR data is both the source for historical reporting as well as predictive-analytics-based forecasting.

Weblog Data: E-commerce is another source of significant amount of data for the airline. Again, for a $1 billion–revenue airline, it could be in the range of tens of thousands of transactions recorded in the weblog daily. These weblogs are gold mines of information about customers and the online journey that took them to the airline's website. If collated and tapped well, there could be significant learnings from weblog data. Learnings could be used to improve sales channel effectiveness, customer analytics, and products rather than just for commercial reporting or forecasting, as used today.

Social Media Data: Since the advent of Facebook and Twitter, there have been increasing interactions between airlines and customers through social media. These interactions give a significant opportunity for the airlines to shape various aspects of their product and service and execute operational functions such as customer service. While this generally cannot be used for quantitative modeling or reporting, there is significant commercial value to be derived from customer sentiment analytics and the adjustments needed to drive increasing brand value.

4.2   BIG DATA USES IN AIRLINE COMMERCIAL PROCESSES

There are at least five main uses of Big Data as practiced today in most companies that could be useful for airlines. The below sections discuss these cases in detail.

4.2.1   PRODUCT/SERVICE IMPROVEMENT

Big Data sourced from social media and online ratings is becoming an important way to improve product and service offerings at many airlines and travel companies. But there are caveats to what can be done with social media data. It is voluntary and hence may be coming from a self-selected group of feedback providers. It is also not comprehensive as it does not include information from customers not on social media.

Nevertheless, airlines and travel industry companies are beginning to leverage social media data to steadily improve their products and services. To illustrate its usage, let's consider how a major airline might go about doing this, as the below example shows.

A large global airline has a well-established route network and service operation in place and is focused on increasing commercial performance and profits. This airline has a well-defined social media function in place. It is currently using social media mainly for customer service and brand building. We believe many airlines would be in this category today as they are not able to push their social media usage and gains beyond the basic levels.

The opportunity is in harnessing this data to improve the product and service continuously. Social media inputs are unstructured and continuously streaming in real time. The airline is receiving feedback about their products and services through this channel. They need to use text analytics and first convert this unstructured data to structured data. Once this step is done, it is essential to bring in customer structured data to add color and dimensionality to the imported unstructured data.

The airline may learn the following type of signals:

- Top-tier FFP customers may be telling the airline that NYC LON service levels in the airport lounges are dropping.
- Students may be telling the airline that deals and services offered to students by the airline are not competitive.
- Elder travelers may be telling the airline that they like to turn to competitor airlines X and Y for vacation packages as they are more reliable for giving them the best deals.

- Corporate travelers may be telling the airline that they use the airline for business travel but other airlines for personal travel with their families.

These are powerful insights. Today the data carrying these insights are coming into the airline but are being lost along the way as there are no clear data planning, stewardship, and analytics to derive these insights and present them to the decision makers.

So how can the airline use these insights to improve on their products and services on a continuous basis?

> Once structured customer data are mixed with social media data, the next step is to make this mix richer by adding in all the other dimensionality of structured data such as channels, segments, POS, routes, and time to give the full structured context to the original unstructured streaming data that is coming in. What emerges is a clear signal coming from the streaming social media inputs about the products/services in the various dimensions.

The airline would have to be careful not to go overboard in using the insights and making big changes. The right approach is to establish a process for continuous improvement based on social media insights. They could start a series of conversations throughout their commercial management structure to harness these insights and be on a journey of continuous improvement. These conversations made possible using unstructured data, structured data, and predictive analytics would lead to an understanding of the long-term impact of these changes. The airline would quantify each change opportunity in terms of long-term impact and value created. As an example, they would be able to quantify the net profitability improvement generated in years one, two, and three of changing and keeping service levels high in the NYC LON route above competition. They would model out the share gain and profit improvement and weigh it against the cost of the improvement. Exactly the same approach would be taken for each of the hypothetical insights (signals) we have provided above.

4.2.2   CUSTOMER SEGMENTATION

Advanced customer analytics needs holistic data to arrive at the right segments. The airline is receiving continuous feed of PNR data from all dimensions in the system. The PNR database is the primary repository of data for customer segmentation as this truly represents all transactions coming in across customer segments along all the dimensions. However, to make this into a rich data set of Big Data useful for segmentation, it much be enriched with attribution as in Figure 11, which showed the two dimensions of Big Data growth.

We illustrate this by showing how Frequent Flyer Program (FFP) information can be added to the PNRs as attribution. The PNR contains the customer FFP reference number. The FFP database has rich information on each customer who has signed up for the program. We can match the PNRs and the FFP database and enrich the PNR database with critical customer data. Going the distance, the full spend and earnings from each PNR should also be built into the PNR attribution before advanced analytics modeling. This allows for quantification of long-term value, which should be a significant basis for the customer segments. What emerges then is a clear signal of customer segments and the emerging breaking trends across the sales channels. The airline may be learning the following types of (hypothetical) insights from Big Data segmentation:

- The traditional understanding of profitability of segments is wrong. A highly valued top-tier FFP segment may be less valuable in the long term than some lower-tier segments. This may be true in only certain POS. Advanced analytics will reveal for which POS this is true.
- True value-based segmentation leads to an overhaul of traditional segmentation. Commonly understood segments separated by fare rules are now not in existence. They have been replaced by value-based segments.
- The corporate segment is highly valuable when coming through the GDS channel. But when corporate segments use online booking tools, they drop significantly in valuation as they avail significant pricing discounts when booking through direct channels.

- Call centers receive a large number of calls from corporate segments for travel changes, and this causes profitability of that segment to be down significantly.

4.2.3   CAMPAIGNS AND PROMOTIONS

Airline commercial departments are regularly running promotions to gain market share, drive higher revenues, and increase profits. These tactical promotions create varied impacts, and while some are successful, others many may not produce the desired results. With the advent of Big Data analytics, airlines now have an opportunity to create powerful models to understand how to make promotions yield better results. Rich promotion information is coming in streaming PNR data as well as social media and weblog data.

Big Data contains vital information in real time about tactical promotions running in the organization. This allows for precise modeling of crucial promotion metrics such as visits, queries, bookings, revenues, and profits. All this is coming at volumes and speeds that are not being tapped currently to reinforce with the commercial department to drive success.

The spend and earn from promotion campaigns should be built into the PNR-level attribution before modeling to understand promotions. This allows for quantification of long-term value, the right perspective for evaluating promotions. What emerges then is a clear signal of responses to promotions and campaigns across the sales channels. The airline may be learning the following types of hypothetical insights from Big Data analytics on campaigns and promotions:

- About 75 percent of discount based promotional campaigns result in long-term loss of profitability for the airline
- Cost of Sale (COS) based promotions are 80 percent more likely to deliver positive profitability results.
- The airline is running a discount promotion to 20 percent of its customer base at any given time.
- Two out of three promotions do not result in share gains that are sustainable beyond the three-month window after the promotion has completed.

The reader will note that every promotion may not lead to such conclusions as the above examples. These are merely showing what advanced analytics can reveal, which today's departmental systems cannot.

4.2.4 PRICE OPTIMIZATION

Airline commercial departments are continuously changing prices in the marketplace and reacting to price changes by competition. These are in part driven by automated price changes from the revenue management tools as bookings and inventory positions are changing across the network of flights. They are also reacting to competitor price points, which may be triggered by similar inventory and bookings positions on their flights. These are millions of price point changes across the network and across dimensions. The information about prices for flights across the network is coming from internal and external sources. Company prices are from the reservation systems and competitor prices come from GDS or aggregators such as ATPCO.

Understanding the impact of pricing moves by the airline and by competition is one of the most complex modeling exercises in the commercial enterprise. Many RM and pricing systems have been attempting to do this for decades, but have not been able to deliver a good system that is consistent, responsive, and accurate. With the advent of Big Data analytics, airlines now have an opportunity to create powerful models to understand how and where pricing opportunities exist to yield better results. The airline may be learning the following types of hypothetical insights using Big Data analytics on pricing moves:

- About 75 percent of the pricing discounts result in long-term loss of profitability for the airline.
- Price increases supported by competition are 80 percent more likely to deliver positive profitability results.
- The airline is running a pricing discount campaign to 20 percent of its customer base at any given time.
- Two out of three pricing actions do not result in share gains that are sustainable beyond the three-month window after the promotion has completed.

Again, the above examples are merely showing what advanced analytics can reveal, which today's departmental systems cannot.

4.2.5   OPERATIONAL EFFECTIVENESS

Airline commercial departments are making multiple decisions every day at all levels in their operations. The decisions are (presumably) made on information provided to the decision-makers through systems, reports, and dashboards. The effectiveness of the commercial organization depends critically on the quality and effectiveness of their information-delivery process. Organizations that excel in these information-delivery processes have a significant competitive advantage. Their systems, reports, and dashboards are wired to be delivered with low latency (closeness to real time), with higher accuracy, and with better insights. Advanced analytics systems deliver a step function improvement in providing timely insights on operations compared to traditional BI systems.

> But the key to advanced analytics, which separates it from straight-up business intelligence, is predictive modeling. The data science within advanced analytics is all about modeling that delivers forecast of outcomes based on drivers. It models how drivers are shaping up and impacting the future. It presents scenario modeling as various options to change the future by changing the drivers of results. This is the most significant advantage the commercial department can be given to execute because it allows the freedom to choose the course of actions knowing their impact on results. This is Analytics 3.0.

Multidimensional Demand Forecasting with Advanced Analytics
A big advantage of analyzing data across channels, POS, and flights in real time using predictive analytics is the capability to accurately forecast demand across these dimensions. Accurate demand forecasting across dimensions increases the overall effectiveness of the commercial department.

It uses all the data coming in at the volumes and speeds at which the patterns are shifting and signals changing. It then models how the drivers represented by these data are shaping the outcomes and predicts it accurately. It can also deliver scenario modeling and what-if analyses. Finally, it has the ability to recommend the optimal driver values that will generate the highest margins. Knowing all this is powerful. The operations of the company will increase manifold and permanently with such power.

Real-Time Business Intelligence for Operational Effectiveness

With streaming Big Data and predictive analytics, latency in reporting is significantly reduced in high-performing airlines. Reports that take weeks to deliver information on dashboards now get delivered in real time. This is one of the most significant developments in Big Data capabilities that offer core productivity improvements in airlines. All airlines run promotions to increase their bookings and market share. Usually they have to wait days and even weeks to understand the effectiveness of promotions. Knowing how your promotions are turning out in real time can be the difference between profitable and unprofitable promotions. Similarly, airlines run price changes, distribution channel adjustments, and marketing events among thousands of actions they take daily to drive higher bookings and share. Knowing in real time the impact these are having and making critical adjustments is powerful and drives effectiveness.

Cross Functional Process Alignment for Optimal Execution

An important benefit of modern Big Data analytics is the cross functional nature of the analytics. They are designed to act on cross functional data that transcend departmental and functional silos. Whether it is PNR details (structured data), or promotion-response emails or social media data, or call center data from customer calls, they represent actions that are always cross functional in nature. The entire commercial department is working on pieces of process to drive higher bookings, and hence the analytics must bring them all on the same page for the insights.

Using advanced analytics, sales, marketing, and revenue managers are in sync on the signals emerging daily on drivers of bookings, revenues, and profit margins. We can take an example to see how this would work: The sales and RM heads would both be given the *insight* that "there is a pattern of increased bookings of company X from city A to B. This is due to a new office of company X in city A. The HQ of the company is in city B. This should increase the bookings by 15 percent." Knowing this in real time gives both the sales and RM teams the ability to be on the same page and take steps to maximize profit margins. They are now aligned to change the pricing and sales levers to maximize revenues and profit margins coming from X, given this new signal that was picked up and amplified by predictive analytics.

4.3 TRANSACTIONAL BIG DATA FOR PREDICTIVE ANALYTICS

McLaren: Use of Big Data analytics

Racing company McLaren has one of the best examples of modern Big Data analytics for improved decision making. It is impressive because it stands apart in its industry in being the leader of data based analytics. Its cars transmit more than 120 telemetric variables as they race along the tracks. The system works on probabilistic optimization models to recommend to the racing team in real time decisions that give them the best chance of winning the race. Using these cutting-edge analytics, McLaren gives its racing teams an increased chance of winning close races. They have developed a deep expertise that uses real-time Big Data to identify the signal from the noise and produce high-stakes decisions based on modeling. They are so successful that they have started a consulting company to deliver this expertise to many industries, not just the car racing industry. Using Big Data and real time simulation, they are able to advise clients on key decisions for winning performance in wide areas of applications, such as Olympic competition and bicycle manufacturing. They have tapped into Big Data and predictive analytics using optimization, paving the way for a flourishing company and helping may other companies across multiple industries.

Source: http://www.bloomberg.com/news/articles/2014-10-02/mclaren-uses-racing-expertise-in-data-driven-consulting

Box 3: McLaren - a standout example of Big Data predictive analytics

Box 3 shows an example of one of the best uses of Big Data driving predictive analytics and producing great results for companies. McLaren is a racing company but has found a great niche in starting a high tech service focused on Big Data analytics. Airlines can take a page out of McLaren's book to understand how large number of drivers (pun unintended) can be distilled into the most important decisions for winning.

If airlines are to become expert at Big Data analytics like McLaren and deliver the best results, a lot of data preparation is needed to run cross functional, multidimensional regressions. Data preparation is one of the core tasks in harnessing advanced analytics. The more effort that is put into understanding data inputs needed for running regression models, the more successful is the path to harnessing advanced analytics. This is not just an IT function, but a function involving the business and more importantly business leadership, IT leadership, and analytics leadership.

As we transcend conventional business intelligence—data warehouses and reporting—to Analytics 3.0, which includes predictive and prescriptive analytics, significant transformation is needed in the data that feeds these applications. The challenge for Big Data analytics is to record all drivers correctly on each the transactions (bookings). It is a significant amount of work to record the drivers of profit margins and track them accurately along the full booking cycle. This is Big Data at work for advanced analytics. When we drill down and use conditional probabilities for prediction (as most advanced analytics machine learning algorithms would use), we should be able to mark the myriad paths those conditions take toward delivering the profits. Digging deep into the data to record those paths and to quantify the probabilities is the daily hard work needed to make real-time predictions of revenues and profit margins.

The modern version of the data warehouse is the "data lake." This is the huge integration of data taking place at the enterprise level to feed modern analytics models. The characteristics of these data lakes are quite different from those of the erstwhile data warehouses. Data lakes are wired together with ETL processes to serve daily analytics. They are designed to deliver operational and decision-support business intelligence to every layer of the organization unlike the data warehouses of the past, which were mainly for offline analytical processes. *The essential ingredient of this is neither size nor volume, but variety and readiness for advanced mathematical modeling.* This is the key ingredient needed in modern advanced analytics.

Transactional Big Data will feed enterprise analytics models running within various suites, supporting the entire organization in its thousands of decisions daily. These decisions are embedded within the various processes of the enterprise. Every day the models will run and provide forecasts and optimized insights. The predictive analytics drive multiple questions daily from the layers of management tasked with delivering optimal execution. So it is critical to understand and support the scope of the effort to keep the data lakes filling up daily with the right information, allowing the models to provide the right insights to management. Only a joint enterprise-level analytics governance body can understand the scope and support needed for daily processes embedding advanced analytics.

4.4 TAKEAWAYS

- Big Data is not just about volume, variety, and velocity of new data. It is about both new data and complexity added to existing data with new states reached.
- Big Data is both structured data coming from conventional channels and unstructured data coming from new channels
- A significant amount of structured Big Data is residing in Excel spread-sheets across the commercial functions in airlines today. The Excel sheets also have a vast amount of business rules built into manipulating the data to feed models that are used for decision-making.
- Unlocking this Big Data in the Excel sheets and moving it into the enterprise realm with the right governance creates a significant opportunity for airlines to improve the quality and consistency of decision-making.
- Big Data has many applications within airlines to deliver significant value and ROI. Some of the main ones include product and service improvement, promotions that work, dynamic pricing that maximizes revenues, customer segmentation that increases loyalty and CLV, and operational effectiveness that drives down costs by an order of magnitude.
- Using Big Data effectively with modern predictive analytics to forecast and recommend optimal decisions is the key to advanced analytics in airlines. Doing this effectively can have a significant impact on airline profits.
- It is critical to support the scope and effort to feed advanced analytics daily. This is the daily hard work needed to provide enterprise insights to enterprise processes for optimization. Governance is critical in running the daily enterprise advanced analytics and for providing the key ingredient – Big Data.

Five

Coordinated Commercial Analytics

Coming together is a beginning. Keeping together is progress. Working together is success.

—HENRY FORD, INDUSTRIALIST

T he modern airline's commercial department drives revenue for the company through its critical functions of sales, RM, network planning, and marketing. These four major functions within the commercial department are continuously working on delivering the right product, price, promotions, and distribution to maximize the revenue with the least possible cost. The net effect of their actions is to generate revenues through a combination of the highest number of bookings at the highest yield. While the commercial functions are driving the bookings and yields to maximize revenues, margins are elusive and not commensurate with expectations. Alignment of the whole team is needed to drive the highest margins, and that is the focus of this chapter.

5.1   THE CONNECTION BETWEEN COMMERCIAL COORDINATION AND ECONOMIC PROFITS

There is a history of literature about airline economics. There are books, management articles, and consultant opinions on this. But let's visit this again to demystify the reason why airline economics really does not work well to deliver profits to the vast majority of airlines. It is well documented and understood that airlines have very high fixed costs. Their variable costs in sales and distribution (necessary to achieve desired sales) are also quite high. Given the combination of high fixed costs and variable costs, the margins (on a per-unit basis) are very small. The difference between successful and unsuccessful airlines is the few percentage points on the margins. The very best and successful ones manage about 5 percent margins historically.

So what accounts for the better margins that successful airlines are able to consistently deliver compared to the majority of their competition? This is the crux of what we are driving our paradigm shift to address.

There are basically two factors that separate this performance:

1. Simultaneous focus on higher unit revenue and lower unit cost
2. Execution—delivering the highest total margin as a result of this focus

Higher unit revenue is driven by a combination of factors: higher loads and higher yields. This combination of superior performance is very elusive. Only a handful of airlines have been able to achieve this in any consistent way. Airlines that do this well don't just have a superior RM function. They have a superior commercial department comprising four core functions: marketing, network planning, sales, and RM. *Further, these airlines are able to drill down to the source of the economically profitable way for this orchestration — generating consistently profitable transactions.* These are the building blocks of their revenue-production engine, the bookings they generate across the company's POS.

So what do these airlines do that makes their decision-making so effective? They plan better, forecast better, read markets better, price better, incent agencies better, communicate brand better, attract loyalty better—to state some of the more obvious drivers of superior profits.

Understanding economics of transactions is the core building block of advanced analytics. This is fundamentally different from what most systems do today and why it becomes important to go down to the lowest granularity of where profits are being made and show them in all the dimensions where they are occurring. Without capturing this granularity and aggregating it from there, we are missing many facts, and this has profound significance in how we can model the predictive analytics and how profit economics works.

What is clear here is that it takes a complete orchestration of the core commercial functions to drive profits and not just excellence in any one of the commercial functions. This is perhaps the most overlooked aspect of commercial performance for the majority of airlines. Even if organizations realize the importance of all commercial functions, they cannot orchestrate them optimally. Even the most sophisticated airlines function in silos. Why is this the case?

We table below three critical reasons that make departments function in silos:

1 They are focused on too many different metrics.
   • RM focuses on yield, not profit margins of bookings.
   • Sales focuses on sales targets, not profit margins of bookings.
   • NP focuses on aircraft utilization and rotation economics, not profit margins of bookings.
   • Marketing focuses on customer value and brand building, not profit margins of bookings.
2 They lack of an integrated enterprise analytics system (forecasting and optimization) across these functions.
3 They lack an integrated dynamic dashboard application to track and guide decisions.

We will explore each of these reasons in greater detail below and highlight actions to bring the focus back to coordinated commercial execution.

5.2   ACTION 1: FOCUS ON A SINGLE METRIC ACROSS DEPARTMENTS

One of the main reasons for lack of execution is lack of alignment to the ultimate goal while chasing scattered goals. The key goal of a modern airline's commercial department is to drive profits of the airline through higher revenue production at lower cost. The right metric to look at enterprise level is not demand, revenue, yield, or marketing ROI. It is profit margin. The laser focus on this singular metric is the only way the entire commercial department can get aligned and drive results well. We will explain how this can be done.

> The secret to ensuring alignment is to ultimately reduce each action to track profit. Today, most actions within the commercial department are not measured for their profit impact. The reality is that most actions do impact profit, but are not measured for the same. Therein lies the biggest issue and opportunity in aligning the whole commercial department. Unless they are able to quantify profit or profit margin impact of every action, the alignment is not complete.

In Figure 12 we present the key drivers of profit margin across dimensions. The controllable drivers are shown on the far right of the figure. Commercial actions should be quantified in terms of these controllable drivers where the action is taking place, but in fact we find most teams focus on intermediate metrics which are not controllable. Further it is of paramount importance to look at these metrics from various dimensions to understand the differing opportunities across dimensions.

Let's see why multidimensional focus on the controllable metrics of profit margin is critical. In a typical airline today, each functional unit is given a budget target. RM is given revenue targets, which are distributed from network level

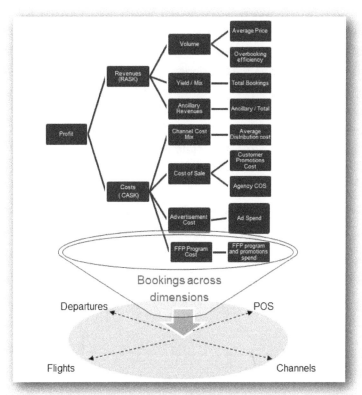

Figure 12: Multidimensional controllable
drivers of commercial profit margins

down to flight level. Sales is similarly given sales targets (not revenue targets), which are distributed from network level to regional level to POS level. Network planning is given mixed targets, not revenue, sales, or profits margins. Marketing is given a spend budget, and its goal is to build brand loyalty and brand value. None of these functions is given a profit margin target. Clearly we can see even at planning stage there is not much alignment.

With the targets set for each department, we can see how execution misalignment starts immediately. Let's start with profit margins as the main target. It is common to find this target explicitly given only to the CCO by the CEO. So when targets of revenue are set for the entire RM department, there are usually no corresponding targets of commercial profit margins. Same goes for sales targets. As a consequence, revenue optimization and sales maximization are efforts that are carried out without heed to the cost of sale associated with those efforts. Hundreds of transactions are executed each day and they are being priced without profit targets directing the decisions.

We take a simple example to show how the strategy-execution gap emerges and how to plug it.

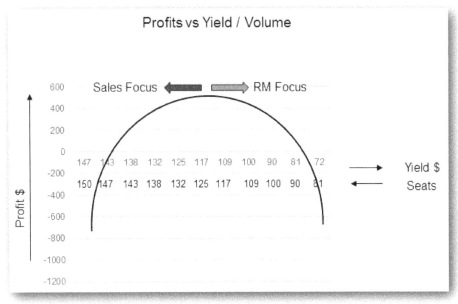

Figure 13: Sales and RM pull in opposite directions

Figure 13 shows an analysis we ran for a client to demonstrate the decision process sales and RM departments go through in driving their agenda. The example is depicting data for a flight that has a capacity of 180 seats. The commercial profit margin for the flight is a function of the revenue and commercial costs. Revenue is driven by volume, which is pursued vigorously by the sales department, and yield, which is pursued by the RM department.

Costs comprise fixed and variable costs including sales and distribution cost. Without an advanced analytics system, this cost information was not available to both the sales and RM teams. So in effect they were not aware of this graph (and therefore at what point in the graph the profit margin is maximized).

This is critical for a number of reasons:

- The sales and RM teams did not have a profit margin target for the flight and were not pursuing the same.
- They did not have a dashboard (or any report) that could inform them of the profit dynamics of this flight with changing volumes and yields.
- They did not have predictive analytics to model the profit margins of the network with changing volumes and yields of this flight.

Yet they were driving their agenda while not being aware of the profit margin impacts of their actions. How did we help them set this right?

We employed advanced analytics techniques using ad-hoc processing. The steps are listed below:

Step 1: Collect fares data by fare class for all classes including the promotional classes.

Step 2: Collect fixed costs attribution data for the flight. This step is difficult, and we have not seen many analyses do this step.

Step 3: Collect the variable cost data for each booking. This is important: this is Big Data at work, and most analyses we have seen do not factor variable costs of each booking.

Step 4: Collate the data—profit margin (fare, cost) of each fare class—against the yield of the fare class and the volume of each fare class.

Step 5: Plot the graph using non-linear-regression analysis.

Step 6: Use the graph to forecast bookings and yield as the flight develops.

Step 7: Fine-tune sales and RM efforts to maximize profits and reach the top of the profit curve for the flight.

While we implemented the above steps on ad-hoc processes, we instituted them in the client's systems with custom solutions. We recommend such process and system changes to embed advanced analytics into the daily execution process.

5.2.1   LACK OF FOCUS—FLOWN REVENUE TARGETS OF RM VERSUS FORWARD SALES TARGETS OF SALES

We want to highlight here the most common misalignment we see in commercial execution – between Sales and RM. At many airlines it is normal to see the sales department having targets of forward sales, while the revenue management department has targets of flown revenue. This may appear to be a perspective and definition problem on the surface and hence is most often overlooked by commercial leadership.

In reality it impacts execution as these critical departments are not laser aligned. This hypothetical example from a client meeting during the CCO's review of May performance is illustrative to understanding target gaps.

It is May, and the revenue performance of the airline is below target. The CCO is asking for reasons. RM is digging into the reasons while sales cannot see the problem because it is beating the May sales targets. The discussion is focused on May flown revenue, which is how the targets are set for RM. There is no report available to quantify how sales leading up to May would result in May flown revenue. The CCO is asking for such a report, and the sales head takes it down as an action item to provide him the report after the meeting. Of course this is not the first time such a discussion is taking place and would certainly not be the last time. Yet, each time it comes up, there is a lack of congruence from sales and RM, and no reports are available to help resolve the questions and aid some decisions.

To remedy this situation, the CEO and CCO must look at commercial department goal congruence very carefully and understand nuances such as flown versus forward sales, which could be causing execution gaps.

5.2.2   POINT OF SALE VERSUS CENTRALIZED TARGET GAPS

Sales departments are generally organized along POS - regions, territories, cities and districts. Every POS generates bookings for flights in the airline's network, and performance is measured against targets set for the bookings. Forward sales targets are spread across the flights that originate in that POS as well as for other flights. The core issue here is that multiple POS are contributing toward the sales on a flight, and dividing up the sales target among these POS is not easily done. Despite difficulties, these targets are still made by the sales head, and he or she produces POS sales targets. These POS sales targets are not translated into flown revenue targets by flights. This is the real problem in POS sales targets and the flown revenue way of measuring performance in an airline. RM and Sales are not talking the same language.

To remedy these gaps, the CCO must solve two issues:

1. Set flown revenue targets in addition to forward sales targets
2. Break down the flown revenue targets by POS at flight and route levels

If the above two steps are done, then the CCO meetings on performance can track target and achievements to targets meaningfully across POS.

5.2.3 NETWORK PLANNING—NOT MEASURED ON COMMERCIAL MARGINS

Network planning and scheduling department make up a very important commercial function. Network planning and scheduling are the functions that basically define the product (in terms of service between cities), the capacity of the flight, and the frequency and timing of the product. Essentially, the route network that is available to be sold by the sales and revenue management functions is defined and put into place by the network planning department.

The revenue production of the modern airline is critically dependent on the product, network, and schedule put together by the NP department and maintained by it 365 days of the year. Yet there are big gaps between the commercial department's core focus on profit margins and the performance metrics used to measure NP.

NP is usually measured on a few key metrics—schedule efficiency, network efficiency, fleet utilization, connectivity and connection times, rotation efficiency, QSI, number of cities served, code share partnerships (though it is more a sales function that drives this), and network traffic flow, among others. These are important metrics, and the VP of the NP department is totally focused on these metrics in all meetings. These important metrics are unfortunately not profit metrics and therefore do not ensure alignment. They are discussed by the CCO in meetings, and NP is part of the discussion. But NP is not measured on the CCO's profit margin metrics.

As part of the CCO's commercial team, NP also should be measured for profit margins. The network and schedule that are put in place should be driving higher profit margins. NP leadership should be given the same target of profit margins as the sales leadership or RM leadership. At each CCO meeting, NP would have to contribute to the discussion of how the full commercial team is driving higher profit margins and what specific NP decisions led to increase or decrease of profit margins. What gets measured gets delivered.

5.2.4   MARKETING—NOT MEASURED ON COMMERCIAL MARGINS

The role of marketing function has evolved significantly after the advent of online and social media marketing. New methods and channels notwithstanding, marketing still has the main role of building brand value of the company, creating long-term demand and loyalty in the market. In pursuing this task, marketing should still be a member of the CCO's commercial team that is driving profit margins.

At most airlines it is difficult today to place a profit margin target for marketing function. At the CCO's meetings, marketing's role is supportive of the main agenda, discussing the profit margins, but not one directly accountable for it. We believe this lack of profit margin accountability in discussing the marketing team's contribution is adding to the lack of coordination in execution.

If we take a project approach, there are many marketing projects that add a lot of value to the airline and of course there are many that don't. Some are allowed to deliver, and others don't get supported to that extent. What we have observed is that very few airlines track marketing decisions, actions, and projects back to profit margin. There is no quantified performance management, and so ROI on marketing spend is difficult to measure. Quantified performance management of marketing would require advanced analytics, and the investment would make marketing deliver a measurable ROI as every other action in commercial does.

5.3   ACTION 2: INTEGRATED ENTERPRISE ANALYTICS SYSTEM

Since the airline deregulation in the United States in 1978, we have seen great progress in commercial functional systems. RM systems deliver inventory-control decision support to the function's analysts. Network planning systems from similar vendors provide good support for NP analysts as they design improvements to the network and explore code share agreements with partner carriers. CRM and sales force automation (SFA) systems provide some good level of support for executing the sales functions. Among the four major commercial functions, marketing is usually the one which does not have a major system supporting its functional analytics.

But even as much as RM, NP, and sales systems have been improving in the last few years, they have not been able to deliver the cross functional coordination needed to take commercial execution to the next level. These systems are fundamentally designed for functional support and do not optimize at the enterprise level across departments and functions. While each of the vendors may suggest their products can optimize across functions, our experience suggests they are not enterprise level advanced analytics solutions.

5.3.1   1990S AND 2000S WITH ERP SYSTEMS

Let's understand this from the perspective of ERP systems that have also been helping organizations manage cross functional execution. Before the advent of ERP systems, most organizations were struggling with executing transactions that spanned functions. There was no common application that could thread a transactional process as it spanned from one department to another. Each department had its own database and application that was different from those of the neighboring departments. Excel spreadsheets, local databases, and custom-built applications proliferated in all departments as a result of this. It resulted in highly uncoordinated execution as these applications did not share information free. For example, order-to-bill was one process that spanned several functions. It was difficult for organizations to track orders between functions and let both internal execution and customers have transparency in the process. It made for very difficult coordination between functions, and execution was suboptimal. ERP systems changed all that.

ERP systems helped organizations with execution of transactions. They were built for cross functional coordination of processes that spanned functions. The database was designed to accommodate the needs of all the departments and feed the single application that spanned functions. Today most of the companies in the Fortune 500 use an ERP system to join together functions seamlessly across processes.

However, ERP systems are not designed for analytics and decision support. These organizations who became expert at managing transactional execution, still find big gaps in decision-making across functions.

With the advancement of Big Data and predictive analytics, there is new urgency in developing systems that will aid in the airline decision-making process and deliver superior profits. Many airlines have started investing in projects that bring advanced analytics capabilities to operations and commercial teams. But these systems are still in their infancy and are not well thought out or built with industry expertise. They tend to be built with local expertise within an airline's IT or operations research team, which is a step in the right direction but very expensive and not optimal. They should use industry-standard products that are pioneering Big Data predictive analytics.

5.4   ACTION 3: INTEGRATED DASHBOARD APPLICATION TO DELIVER DECISIONS

The last piece of the puzzle to ensure commercial coordination in execution is the platform that brings the department together with common insights – a central dashboard. Here, it is important to make a distinction between "single version of insights" and the commonly used description "single version of the truth." What many IT and business intelligence professionals call single version of the truth is very elusive in most airlines (and other industries as well, we believe). It is not enough to just get the right data into the EDW systems and into the reports. Data by itself is not what causes multiple versions of the truth. Data is only one piece of the puzzle in getting to the truth. The intent is to get the right insights to the executives, managers, and analysts who make decisions daily on maximizing profits. Data needs to be modeled for forecasting and optimization of profits. The drivers and forecasted profits (in all the dimensions and in all the granularity) need to be reported as the single version of insights.

For effective cross functional execution, insights have to be pushed to decision-makers when and where they need to be made. Today's processes in airlines span functions and require insights for decisions at every stage of the process. Driving revenues on flights in a profit-maximizing way is essentially a process that spans the entire commercial department and requires myriad decisions along the way. This needs to be supported by commercial enterprise dashboards at all levels in the commercial organization.

Advanced analytics are involved in every stage from planning to execution to performance management reviews. During the planning months, the CCO would chair meetings to kick-start and review the plans. He would have his entire commercial team there in the meetings. The dashboards would need to show the performance metrics across dimensions in the previous years and provide predictive analytics based forecasts of performance in the coming year.

During the planning meetings, the CCO's team would iteratively change the commercial driver mix that produces revenues and profits for the coming year. This would need to be supported in each step by the advanced analytics dashboard, which shows the forecasted profits with what-if analytics.

Once the plans are approved and execution begins, the dashboards would need to support quarterly, monthly, weekly, and daily review meetings by the various commercial teams. Let's look at some of these meetings.

The quarterly and monthly review meetings chaired by the CCO would involve the entire commercial department. They would discuss revenue, cost, and profit targets, and performance against targets. Predictive-analytics-based forecasts of profits for the coming quarters and the full year would also be shown by the dashboards. These metrics would be discussed at each dimensional level, some of which we list below:

- Overall network level
- Regional network level
- Regional level
- POS level
- Channel level
- Customer Segment level
- Quarter, month, week and day level

Using these dashboards, the commercial leadership team would understand emerging risks and opportunities along and across dimensions. This allows for contingency planning to restore profitability in dimensions which are underperforming by optimizing drivers exactly like we showed in the first example in the introduction chapter. The central dashboards would need to support those discussions and decisions.

Coming down a level to the analysts, these dashboards would need to show the same metrics at a much more granular level. For example, an analyst in the pricing department would be shown the future expected profit performance of the flights he is managing. He would further be shown the optimal pricing on these flights based on advanced analytics modeling.

At every level, therefore, the dashboards have the following characteristics:

- They report on cross functional profit generation across dimensions.
- They are real time and take into account the latest developments.
- They are descriptive, predictive, and prescriptive based on advanced analytics modeling running on enterprise data.
- They have smart graphs customized to each member of the commercial department.

We will revisit the topics of dashboards based systems in detail in chapter 8.

5.5 TAKEAWAYS

- Airlines that are able to have superior coordination across RM, sales, NP, and marketing are able to drive higher per-unit revenue and margins.
- Lack of coordination is caused by three main factors: (1) lack of focus on a single metric across the departments, (2) lack of an integrated enterprise analytics system across the departments, and (3) lack of an integrated dashboard system across the departments.
- The lack of alignment between sales and RM is because sales focuses on forward sales while RM focuses on flown revenue. Sales metrics are distributed and divided across POS and channels, while RM targets are distributed across flights and routes, causing the gaps in the metrics.
- ERP systems cut across departmental processes in the 1990s and helped in transactional coordination. What is needed in airlines today is a similarly integrated analytics system for decision coordination and optimization.
- The entire commercial department should be looking at the same dashboards that communicate common metrics in a consistent way. These dashboards always deliver "single version of *insights*."

Six

Advanced Analytics – The CIO Perspective

Now, with more and more data available, businesses are given more opportunity to cherry pick the results they want to see.

—*Nate Silver*

The commercial organization in any airline is the heart of the profit-generation engine. Comprising the core departments of marketing, sales, RM, and planning, it makes the critical decisions that generate demand, set prices, run campaigns, and maximize revenues around the year. The departments generate a significant amount of activity in their processes each day and around the year. The leadership team of the commercial department is responsible for the decisions on these activities. They are continuously looking for analytics to generate insights on taking the right decisions. Yet today they do not have such analytics. All they have are Excel spreadsheets and lots of reports that deliver more uncertainty. What they need is predictive analytics, which allow them insights into the future and clear the path. This chapter focuses on the analytics stack needed to deliver the predictive analytics to management. We further present a playbook for the CEO to set up the analytics stack, process and governance in place.

6.1   GOOGLE ANALYTICS—A GOOD START FOR ENTERPRISE ANALYTICS

Google Analytics is an industry solution that has standardized analytics for the e-commerce function across industries. It has built a stack of standard tools that can be put in place in any organization for collecting and presenting critical e-commerce data, providing abundant data and metrics to users.

The continuum of delivering insights from data is complex to execute. Google Analytics has made it possible to conquer this continuum in part, but is not sufficient to be a complete solution. It cuts across functional silos and integrates data to produce a fine collection of metrics about customers, journeys, products, revenues and profits. These metrics are standardized and are communicated via easy-to-understand screens. Users across industries would recognize the same screens and metrics presented at various levels.

Yet, Google Analytics is not as an enterprise decision tool. First it dwells exclusively on the e-commerce domain - it does not address other channels at present. Second Google Analytics (the standard version) is not a prescriptive analytics tool. It is focused on descriptive analytics, reporting activities of the past. It does not get into the forecasting and optimization aspects of predictive analytics, needed for decisions.

6.2   DEPARTMENTAL ANALYTICS VS ENTERPRISE ANALYTICS

As enterprises are getting used to the quality and availability of Google Analytics' type of capabilities, they are ready for real predictive analytics—enterprise style. This is beyond any single department; it is unifying and optimizing all the functions in the commercial department. We describe it in this section.

Let's contrast departmental analytics and enterprise analytics with an example. We focus on the customer to see how marketing, and sales would run their own analyses in today's departmental analytics, and how they could be using enterprise analytics.

We contrast B2C customers with B2B clients, to understand how marketing and sales usually differ in their focus. Sales seeks to understand B2B clients while leaving the e-commerce and marketing departments to focus on individual segments. Sales pursues client contract modeling and promotions modeling. Marketing claims the main customer ownership. They run customer segmentation analyses and all the modeling around customers, seeking to drill down to individual customers. They pursue customer choice modeling, customer response modeling, and customer score modeling. Both these critical departments source their own data within their own systems and develop these models in Excel and take decisions within their functions. The important point to note is that these decisions are not discussed and agreed upon by a common understanding. As a result, B2C and B2B activities are largely uncoordinated, and so are the sales and marketing pursuit of these customers. This is the biggest problem with the way departmental analytics works and hinders an enterprise-level unification of customer pursuit. This has significant revenue implications which can be optimized!

In the enterprise analytics world, marketing and sales would have more seamless interaction, sharing of data and insights. They would identify the opportunities common to them, as models are showing this at the enterprise level. They have no disagreements on the models or the data, as these are standard across the enterprise. They just have to jointly understand where the opportunities are in the entire client space, whether it is B2B or B2C, and how they can go after it in unison. All the analytics are common and the decisions are taken together. In the section below, we describe how an airline could arrive at this state of advanced analytics. We describe the stack of technology and processes which deliver enterprise analytics.

6.3 BUILDING BLOCKS—THE FULL PREDICTIVE ANALYTICS STACK

There are many departmental level analytics models and tools, but very few enterprise level analytics tools. We describe in this section a comprehensive set of services that make up the analytics stack for the entire commercial department. Figure 14 shows the stack made of layers, and each layer has a purpose in delivering the service toward enterprise analytics. The brief description of each layer of the stack is on the right side panel of the figure.

Layers 1 and 2: ETL

At the bottom of the stack, but very important to the process are the extract, transform, and load (ETL) services required to perform the critical data integration. Enterprise analytics source data from multiple systems through ETL processes. Layer 1 houses ETL software for sourcing data from external systems (like ATPCO pricing data or industry market share data). Layer 2 houses ETL software for sourcing data from internal systems (like PNR and bookings data from the reservations system or promotions data from Sales systems). We provide a starting list of data sources below for commercial advanced analytics:

- PNR data — Historical bookings on each flight departure (12 -24 months)
- Schedule data – Historical or current schedule data to tie the bookings to schedule flights
- Pricing data – Internal pricing by booking as well as competitive pricing data
- Distribution channels and Cost data — Channel the booking was made and a cost allocation for those channel bookings
- Cost of sale data — contractual and ad-hoc cost associated with bookings
- Promotions data – Promotion codes which drive bookings and the cost associated
- Corporate tour codes – Corporate code associated with the booking showing the client and the cost for that booking
- FFP data – FFP tiers of the booking customer and also the allocated cost of the FFP program by tier and any special promotional cost of the FFP booking.

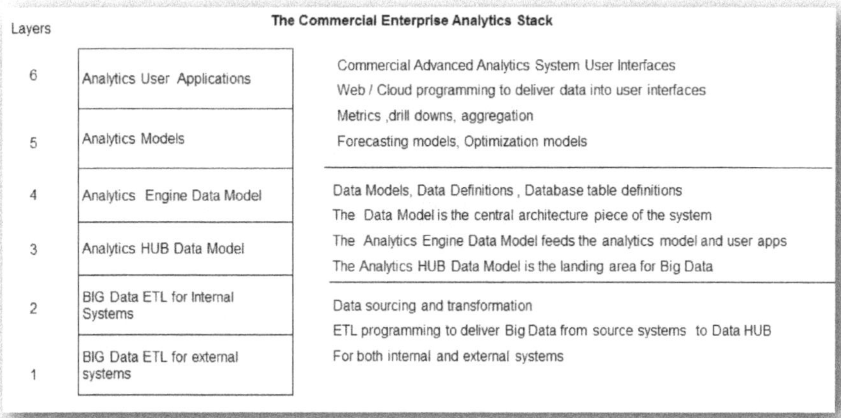

Layers	The Commercial Enterprise Analytics Stack	
6	Analytics User Applications	Commercial Advanced Analytics System User Interfaces Web / Cloud programming to deliver data into user interfaces
5	Analytics Models	Metrics ,drill downs, aggregation Forecasting models, Optimization models
4	Analytics Engine Data Model	Data Models, Data Definitions , Database table definitions The Data Model is the central architecture piece of the system
3	Analytics HUB Data Model	The Analytics Engine Data Model feeds the analytics model and user apps The Analytics HUB Data Model is the landing area for Big Data
2	BIG Data ETL for Internal Systems	Data sourcing and transformation ETL programming to deliver Big Data from source systems to Data HUB
1	BIG Data ETL for external systems	For both internal and external systems

Figure 14: A modern commercial enterprise analytics stack

The ETL processes populate databases that power the analytics layers. In the airline and travel industry, the PNR is the critical system of record at a transactional level. By increasing the attribution on a PNR record, the activities of the commercial department can be tracked on the PNR. The information needed to run the sophisticated modeling in the analytical model layers is built into this layer. The following is a subset of the programming we will see in this layer:

- Preparing stochastic demand buildup for a flight departure, organized along reading days
- Attributing dimensionality to demand such as POS, customer segment, and channel
- Organizing demand by dimensions
- Attributing COS to demand, such as sales channel cost and promotions cost
- Attributing cost of distribution to demand, such as GDS cost and POS distribution cost
- Attributing loyalty index and loyalty program cost to demand
- Attributing social media feedback into transactions

Layers 3 and 4: Data Model

The data model is the central architecture of the enterprise predictive analytics system. This has to be inclusive, carefully designed, and flexible to allow for the massive possibilities in the layers above to deliver enterprise-wide predictive analytics. The problem with most operational and analytical systems of today is that their data models are not inclusive, flexible, or extensible to allow for the future possibilities. Hence this becomes the most crucial part of the analytics stack. It is the heart of the system. It guides what happens in the layers above and below. The following are some of the data that would be captured in these data models:

- Transaction records with full attribution, including dimensionality and cost elements
- Multidimensional input and output data for all analytics models
- Optimization input and output data
- Aggregated dimensional profit drivers and profit margins
- All the above organized by time dimension, forward and backward looking
- Secondary and tertiary drivers of results, such as load factors, bookings, events, GDP, etc.

The data models should allow for dimensional and driver attribution to be overlaid on the core transactions in real time. This lends itself to a typical format used in many Enterprise Data Warehouses (EDW) called the star schema. The data model will consist of the core transaction table which houses all the PNR transactions. As transactions are added daily, they incrementally increase the transaction set. Needless to say, very old data records will be archived. Dimensional information will be stored and updated to keep them current. They are separate from the transactional tables for ease of maintenance. As this serves advanced analytics with real time insights, programs are working continuously behind the scenes updating the transaction tables with dimensional and driver information. While it appears that today's EDWs do similar processing, the difference is that advanced analytics ETL needs to be in real time and not weeks or days late as today's EDWs deliver. This impacts their usefulness for real time analytics.

The ETL processes and data models are very specific to airlines and use significant business rules in delivering the data needed. They cannot be performed by generic consulting and products. The CIO will note the need to put together a real talented team to deliver this service towards the predictive analytics stack.

Layer 5: Analytical Models

The upper layers are housing the critical predictive analytics models, which distinguish this stack from traditional BI and descriptive analytics. The predictive analytics models use historical data from various systems to derive signals, forecast scenarios and outcomes. They further optimize the outcomes and provide clear insights to the users where the actions are needed to deliver the optimal results. At the core they are revenue opportunity models.

The core analytical models drive the forecasting and optimization engines. Traditional time series forecasting models use extrapolation techniques to project past trends onto the future. These techniques, such as exponential smoothing, do not explicitly model drivers but rely on trends to forecast demand. But in order to extract the signal from the noise in a more meaningful way, we must make advances in forecasting, and employ modern techniques based on causal forecasting. Predictive analytics forecasting models that use regression (a causal forecasting method) have become more common, and they are likely to produce more accurate results. The latest predictive models use machine learning techniques, which, when combined with Big Data, deliver a significant improvement in forecasting capabilities.

The analytical models in enterprise analytics work on enterprise-wide drivers of demand, revenue, and profit margins. This is a separating feature of enterprise analytics compared with departmental analytics. Profits in the airline industry are generated by actions across the whole airline in driving up revenues and driving down costs. Revenues and cost drivers are spread across the airline but act in unison to deliver the profits. Unless we model them as such—which is the way enterprise analytics does—we would be assessing the effects of these drivers in pieces, and it does not work that way in reality.

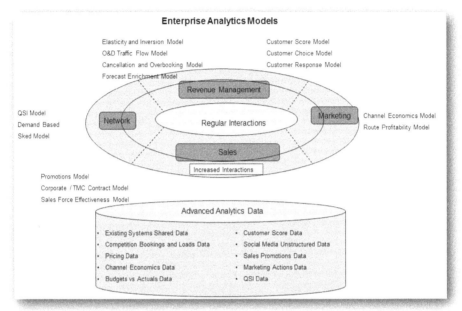

Figure 15: Enterprise analytics commercial models and data in a modern airline

In Figure 15 we show enterprise analytics models for the commercial department, and explain how they are distinct from the functional versions of the same:

Each of the above models is primarily running in one of the four commercial functions today. In enterprise predictive analytics, they are running *for* every department *but modeled and optimized at the enterprise level*. This is a crucial point to observe and remember.

Let's look at the pricing inversion model to illustrate how departmental analytics transform to enterprise analytics to deliver value. The purpose of the inversion predictive analytics model is to show future instances where yield is dropping instead of increasing. Today there is no question this belongs totally within the walls of the pricing and revenue management department. Sales, network planning, and marketing have usually no direct responsibility in running analytics that show pricing inversions and making decisions around it (though we have seen pro-active sales departments do this). But if we look deep into pricing inversion, how to model the analytics, and how to take decisions, we find why it belongs in the enterprise realm.

The price charged for bookings is determined by the pricing department, and the availability is determined by the RM department. But marketing has a big role to play in determining the ultimate average price extracted from the market. So does the sales department. Marketing creates demand in the medium to long term while sales is focused on the short to medium term. It would be just as relevant for the marketing team to understand the price inversion caused by demand creation as it would be for the pricing and RM teams. The difference is that marketing may not be looking at it on a per-flight basis, but at an aggregated level. Similarly, Sales efforts are focused on short-term demand creation. They could be running promotions across flights and regions, and this could be leading to some pricing inversion on flights being tracked by pricing and RM teams. So with this example we see how the actions of all departments need to be modeled together. The same is the case for all other models, which are all in fact enterprise models.

Layer 6: The Analytics User Applications Layer

This layer presents the insights of the predictive analytics to end users. It takes the results from the models layers and transforms them as needed at any level and function. This layer critically depends on the data model to be highly effective to be able to harness the predictive model insights and present them meaningfully to end users.

What distinguishes this from traditional BI is twofold: (1) the results are based on predictive modeling; and (2) the information is dynamic in nature, enabling interactive scenario analyses. Underlying both these features is the intelligence built into the stack through advanced analytics. Further this is at enterprise level ensuring that no department has monopoly over either the data or methods used in deriving the insights.

6.4 BUILDING THE PREDICTIVE ANALYTICS STACK – A PLAYBOOK

6.4.1 NOT HAVING ADVANCED ANALYTICS IS NOT AN OPTION ANYMORE

> We have illustrated that marketing and sales departments are in the demand-creation business as much as pricing and RM teams are in the pricing business—all are contributing to the revenue generated on flights, revenue generated through customer segments, and revenue generated through promotion campaigns. Hence they are all equally invested in understanding pricing analytics over time on their respective dimensions. Thus the modeling should be at the enterprise level.

Advanced Analytics at enterprise level is not commonly found in most companies. Within Airlines, there are very few examples of the type of analytics we have described so far in this book. It will take a visionary CEO to work with the business and IT effectively to get the predictive analytics stack in service. Airlines that have such a system in the future will have a disproportionate advantage to deliver value to their shareholders.

Imagine a competitive airline today without an RM system. Imagine further that all the decisions around managing the flights' revenues are being done through excel spreadsheets. This was the reality before RM systems were introduced in the 1980s. Today nearly all airlines have an RM system (mostly procured, but some homebuilt). If they do not have one, they are not competitive.

Advanced analytics systems are similar to RM systems. Yet as we have noted in chapter 3, RM systems are not decision support systems providing insights to management. Most commercial management today use excel spreadsheets with questionable data and models running them. By using these analytical tools, it is equally possible that a commercial leader may get the decision right or wrong. This chance is being repeated daily over thousands of decisions the commercial leadership teams make. They would need a system that helps them continuously improve the chances of making the right decisions. Considering the impact of these decisions and the need for increased performance effectiveness, we believe it is not optional for airlines to execute without an advanced analytics system in the future. We show below a playbook form how to get such a system in place at the earliest. It is not very difficult, considering the advantages to be had.

6.4.2   THE ENTERPRISE ANALYTICS PLAYBOOK

CEO and CCO establish the business case for advanced enterprise analytics
A significant starting point in having commercial enterprise analytics is for the CEO and CCO to make the business case. Similar to the RM advantage, advanced analytics can deliver about 5% improved performance as noted earlier. This potential advantage is being ignored by almost all airlines as they are playing a zero-sum game at this point with just RM analytics. Stage 5 airlines, leaders in adopting advanced analytics, will reap the benefits and add significant shareholder value. This is something the CEO and CCO must develop as the basis for the advanced analytics journey.

Establish governance for advanced analytics
Once the business case is established, the CEO must set a strict timetable for delivering this capability to the airline. We believe the competitive advantage is significant, and organizations should focus on having it available this year in a matter of months—maybe two to three months. After this, the chief analytics officer (CAO), the chief commercial officer (CMO), and the chief information officer (CIO) get together and institute a governance body (see section 7.4 on governance) to deliver on the CEO's mandate for enterprise predictive analytics.

Make the Build Vs Buy decision
The governance body makes a significant decision on build versus buy of the predictive analytics capability, which we believe is the fundamental decision of the predictive analytics journey, separating success from failure. For most companies, a buy decision is perhaps the right one as far as enterprise analytics goes.

The enterprise predictive analytics stack is a significant system very similar in scope to enterprise BI, EDW and ERP projects (albeit with much different capabilities). We have observed that BI and EDW projects have among the highest rates of failed projects. Enterprise analytics falls under this category. According to a recent article in CIO magazine, about 50% of IT projects will fail[xi]. Other leading industry research organizations like Gartner have similar statistics supporting this view.

We can contrast BI's lack of success with the success of RM systems, which are for the most part buy decisions. It is interesting to study why these two types of systems have vastly different success rates. This may be key to ensuring a high ROI on advanced analytics.

Airline leaders who make the decision to build predictive analytics capability with the help of their IT departments should be aware of the statistic we quoted above from CIO magazine. Many airlines are building significant teams of data scientists and statisticians. While they are impressive and bring a lot of intellectual and mathematical power to these airlines, they do not necessarily lead to high ROI on building analytics systems.

It is our view that products made by market players, if tailored to meet the needs of the airline industry, are best suited for the industry. Airlines continuously pursue profits in a vigorously competitive market, and large IT investments with low probabilities of delivering the ROI are not advisable. Building predictive analytics systems that optimize at the enterprise level is a risky proposition for most airlines.

The CEO and CCO should focus on procuring advanced analytics systems from an industry vendor and build a strong team capable of world-class business analytics. Pursuit of Business Analytics excellence rather than Data Science excellence is the way for airlines to move from good to great. We don't mean to say data science is not critical, but only want to emphasize that it can be largely bought and instituted in a system. That is the way of the future. However, business analytics capabilities cannot be captured in a system The business analytics team should place a premium on understanding the trends and taking the best decisions, not on putting together the data processes to present the trends. An important focus difference which we believe is crucial to analytics success and competitive advantage.

> Its critical to distinguish business analytics from data science here. We have observed many departments develop an overload of data scientists who are experts in statistics, modeling and programming. All of that should be outsourced to the procured advanced analytics system. Such a system would have the models built in to handle diverse data and output metrics. Spending to actually build the models and validate them is again a low ROI activity. We would recommend that business analysts work with end users to identify and communicate advanced analytics metrics and model requirements. If the above suggestions are followed well, it could result in very quick implementations.

Industry vendors have been slow to come out with advanced analytics products for the commercial airline enterprise. RM systems have been tweaked to deliver enterprise analytics capabilities, but lack the DNA of enterprise advanced analytics systems. Specialist consulting companies like Accenture, IBM, Dell and others have introduced more tailored advanced analytics solutions. It would still be a challenge to find a completely tailored solution (like an RM system) for advanced commercial analytics in the airline industry. Industry analyst Gartner presents a wonderful annual report on advanced analytics vendors and classifies them into 4 quadrants. We present in Figure 16 their report from 2016.

Figure 16: Gartner Advanced Analytics Platform vendors 2016
Source (Gartner, Feb 2016 www.gartner.com)

It is interesting to note that none of the traditional airline industry RM vendors finds a place on this graph, which is the case we are making in this book. Advanced enterprise analytics is new to the airline industry and the dedicated vendors need to develop these solutions.

So given there are no fully developed solutions (other than the one we pointed to) of advanced predictive analytics, how does the airline CIO deliver it to the airline? We believe there would have to be a collection of best-of-breed components of the various layers we described in section 6.3. The IT and Business teams would have to get familiar with the details in the stack and bring these solutions together. Advanced analytics consulting expertise from the market would be required to help the internal teams bring this together. It starts resembling a build solution rather than a buy solution. Hence we are urging the industry vendors to develop complete solutions of advanced commercial analytics.

Implement the system as soon as possible – within one quarter

Most large scale IT projects take years to implement, stabilize and start showing value to the users. This is just not advisable in the realm of advanced analytics and what it can mean to the company. Since they can deliver real competitive advantage and the best decision insights on a daily basis, senior management should view advanced analytics systems with a completely different urgency. The governance mandate should be to have this system up and running in months if not weeks. From start to finish, the entire project should be completed within one quarter. Is this possible? We explore below how to ensure this can be done.

We have listed in section 6.3 data sources needed in an advanced analytics system. The governance team will require the CIO to work with all departments to provide this data to the advanced analytics implementation team. This is one of the gating factors for most systems vendors of advanced analytics systems. Procured advanced analytics systems should be able to handle most of the other programming requirements in the analytics stack. The UI and Models layers require analysts to work with leaders at the enterprise level to establish the metrics and the underlying predictive models.

Figure 15 shows a good number of models that will be run in the advanced analytics systems. We have defined many of these models in chapters 9 and 10. Senior management and business analysts work with vendors of the systems to define the models, metrics and UI. Governance will ensure that the procured systems are thoroughly tested and implemented.

Redesign the decision making process to run simple

With advanced analytics powering enterprise insights for decisions, the CEO and CCO will authorize the governance structure to change decisions processes. Meetings at all levels across the commercial department would be required to use enterprise insights from the advanced analytics systems. The introduction to the book started with this concept. It is a powerful paradigm shift in how advanced analytics changes interactions among the commercial department functions. They all use the same system and it produces all the analytics needed for effective cross-functional decisions.

Have ongoing governance of results

The C-Suite, which includes the Chief Analytics Officer, is the parent of the advanced analytics system. It envisioned and put the system in place. Once in place, guidance is provided so that it can produce the right results. This is the single most effective weapon the CEO can develop to gain competitive advantage and drive shareholder value.

6.5   TAKEAWAYS

- Google Analytics is a great place to start understanding how modern enterprise predictive analytics should work. It works without significant IT effort to gather all the data. The enterprise analytics stack is a product tailored to deliver advanced analytics across all commercial functions and should be as easy to implement and use as Google Analytics.
- Enterprise-level predictive analytics for the airline commercial function brings together the data, modeling, and insights across the key departments of sales, RM, network planning, and marketing. In today's world, these functions source their own data, build their own models, and of course derive their own insights, mostly within the stovepipes of their functions, not connected with the other functions.
- Delivering enterprise predictive analytics requires significant work to bring the data, modeling, and user applications together. These three ingredients can be represented as a stack of technologies bringing together the analytics.
- The Predictive Analytics stack comprises 3 main layers of the stack – data integration layers which source regular and Big Data into the databases, an all- important data models layer which integrates the data and massages it to suit all types of enterprise models and finally the models layer which drives the enterprise insights.
- Business leaders can commission vendors or the IT departments in delivering the predictive analytics stack to the commercial department.
- The CEO and CCO should use a playbook (summary in the appendix) to implement an advanced analytics culture and deliver breakthrough results. A critical part of the playbook is a build vs buy decision on the best way to get the analytics in place. Looking at past success of industry products like RM and ERP systems and the past failures of home-made systems like BI systems, we recommend that advanced analytics should be procured and not built ground up.

- A focus on business analysts is more important than building up on data scientists and statisticians. Results orientation of analyses is more important than the ability to understand the arcane math behind the models. This is being overlooked at a majority of commercial and IT departments of many airlines.

Seven

Optimal Execution with Advanced Analytics

Dear CEO, when you get tired of telling the strategy storyline you have reached 3 percent of your target population.

—ANONYMOUS

We do not know how to manage the knowledge worker so that he wants to contribute and perform. But we do know that he must be managed quite differently.

—PETER DRUCKER, 1960

Modern analytics requires management execution to be suitably altered to drive results. Execution is the ability to transform vision, insights, and strategies into results. We have observed that many airlines have clearly defined strategies and planning processes but cannot consistently translate those into profits commensurate with the strategy expectations.

This problem of execution—inconsistent results to expectations of planning and strategy—is one faced by most companies. As with leadership in every industry, management of the airline industry is also very much puzzled by this conundrum. In this chapter, we will break down the main elements of what is needed to get execution right in light of advanced analytics capabilities of organizations.

7.1   THE GAP BETWEEN STRATEGY AND EXECUTION

In their popular book *Execution*, Ram Charan and Larry Bossidy[xii], say execution bridges the gap between promises and results. Strategy can be both the building blocks of the long-term plan and the weapon to win in the marketplace. The best talent is usually deployed to set strategy and not for delivering the results. Despite the abundant emphasis on strategy, the level of execution remains below expectations for most companies. By embracing advanced analytics, airline executives have the opportunity to reduce and even eliminate this gap.

The airline industry is truly a dynamic industry globally. While the biggest growth is being experienced in Asia, the US and European markets are also very dynamic competitive marketplaces. Within these markets, there are microsegments where capacity, demand, price, costs, and profits are continuously changing. There are a significant number of pricing moves and countermoves by each airline and its competitors, creating demand and market share swings. Every day airlines are introducing discounts and tactical promotions within market microsegments, altering the dynamics there. Events are announced daily and demand swings are observed as traffic is drawn by these events. Corporations are changing their travel patterns as they expand and shift their zones of operations, throwing up changes to patterns of corporate travel. A very dynamic marketplace around the globe.

The above notwithstanding, there appears to be industry level predictability of performance and share. Strategies are set with the expectations of a predictable ((not necessarily static) marketplace. They are for the most part forecasting a scenario and results in that scenario. Dynamic strategies planned for multiple outcomes based on real options are rare. Even if airlines do have them, tracking and changing halfway during execution seems impossible given today's capabilities in systems and processes.

Commercial strategies focus on driving higher revenues, lower costs, and ultimately more profits margins. They are developed in annual planning or other review meetings around the year. The execution period for these strategies are often much longer than assumptions of time periods when environments are static. We believe unless advanced analytics are used to create dynamic strategies, execution gaps emerge immediately after strategy sessions are done.

It gets interesting to see how things pan out during the execution phase. There is one critical process going on during that phase, and that is bookings buildup across dimensions. As bookings are building up, they are subject to the realities of competitor price moves, customer demand pattern changes, industry capacity changes, and so on. These are shaping the profit margins of the bookings and may be steering them away significantly from the desired outcomes. Is this not to be expected? Yes, but the planners have not predicted the direction these forces are changing the bookings coming in. (Today's planning systems and processes do not have such advanced predictive analytics capabilities).

We see two key drivers of execution gaps:

1. Strategies are made without real options as execution gaps begin to appear. Airlines usually do not have alternate scenarios mapped out and did not have contingency plans in place for Plan B or Plan C if the strategy was not working out.
2. Management teams very often do not know where they are during execution and what the results are likely to be. There are no predictive analytics systems to guide them in dynamic execution. Therefore, they lack the insights on the correct actions to correct course and get back on track to execute on their strategy. This is usually the bigger reason for execution failure.

Combined, the above two reasons are the biggest drivers of the strategy to execution gap in airlines.

To address this would be a top priority for airline managements worldwide. It would require a business process reengineering of the commercial function. Specifically, the reengineering should be focused on the following aspects:

- Development of enterprise analytics capabilities in the commercial function
- Development of enterprise insights to guide the strategy and execution process
- Institution of governance for enterprise analytics

Let's explore each of these key steps involved in enabling better execution.

7.2 DEVELOPMENT OF ENTERPRISE ANALYTICS CAPABILITIES IN COMMERCIAL

Airlines today have the opportunity to improve revenue and profit performance by a step function through the application of advanced analytics to their commercial strategy and execution process. Here we lay out how to develop deep analytics capabilities of commercial teams.

Many airlines develop analytics capabilities in bits and pieces when they execute specific projects either with internal resources or with the help of consultants. This is fine as a proof of concept that advanced analytics can drive value. But to drive sustainable long-term value in the airline for shareholders, advanced analytics capabilities must be pervasive and sustained.

The analytics capability then must be developed with a business and system architecture that is reliable and always available with insights for the user community. In Figure 17 we show the business and system architecture of the commercial department in a modern airline developing these capabilities.

The diagram illustrates how the new advanced analytics system would empower management and operational teams with insights. The right way for companies to operate is to provide *all* insights to management and then through the governance process get execution to work. Today at most companies, this management concept is a paradox. While they are authorized to deliver results through the governance process, they are not empowered with insights to ensure execution. This creates imbalance. The architecture we show changes this imbalance. It shows the advanced analytics system as a broad block on top, designed to span all commercial functions at the enterprise level. This system feeds decision insights to management top down. The figure further shows operational blocks at the lower level, that feed insights bottom up across the management chain. With this architecture, insights are available across the whole commercial organization to align and drive the right decision every time.

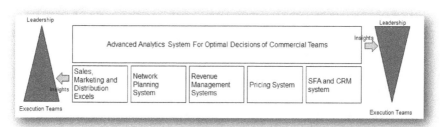

Figure 17: Business and System architecture of commercial advanced analytics

The salient features about this architecture are summarized below:

- Existing commercial systems—sales, RM systems, pricing systems, CRM and NP systems—will continue to be in place as they are critical to running the operations and providing insights to the execution teams.
- The advanced analytics system would be a modern Big Data–based analytics system that sits on top of the existing functional commercial systems by being at the enterprise level (see chapter 6 for a detailed description of the analytics system stack).
- The advanced analytics system would continuously pipe insights to management, empowering them to guide the entire commercial team.
- These insights would be available anywhere, anytime. They would be deployed through intuitive dashboards that always convey the necessary insights with consistent messaging (see chapter 8 on dashboard design).

7.3 DEVELOPMENT OF ENTERPRISE INSIGHTS TO GUIDE EXECUTION

Senior management at most airlines follow the traditional hierarchical way of driving businesses. They have periodic meetings, which would be daily, weekly, monthly, quarterly, and annual meetings. The invitees to these meetings are generally at top level or one level below. Typical discussion points would be company performance, expected performance, and strategy to deliver according to plan. Usually these meetings are conducted with historical reports and very little predictive reports. Some of the larger airlines may have centralized finance and economics teams that provide reports to departments for forecasting. These reports may find their way into the management meetings. The reports used to run management meetings are thus largely historic and with a light future projection based on past performance. We list the main drawbacks in these reports:

- They are derived from BI systems without predictive and prescriptive analytics capabilities, making them backward looking
- They are derived from Excel spreadsheets lacking data quality and governance.
- They are usually tailored to a specific audience for answering specific questions. They do not have flexibility to address unplanned questions.

The last point is crucial for us to understand why most management meetings are run unsuccessfully. Because most reports are prepared using one-way aggregations, they cannot easily serve the purpose of free flowing two-way conversations in business meetings. Let's look at a hypothetical example described in Box 4.

Example – Sales meeting needing two ways flow of insights:

In a management meeting, the executives are given a presentation showing profit margins of the East region sales department, forecast to be 10 percent below targets. The report (on which the presentation is based) is aggregated and does not identify drivers of underperformance. Given the lack of driver details, management would ask the VP of sales to explain why East is below its profit targets. The VP of sales in turn would expect the East region sales manager to provide the correct answer to this question by the management. Here is the other big problem in management meetings: Notice that management's question would be relayed along the hierarchical lines, but the information flow does not follow the same direction. In other words, information flow is coming bottom up, while questions are coming top down. If the East sales manager has done his homework well and is on top of all the insights, he would be able to communicate to the management that competition and lack of demand is driving down profit margins in his region. Management could then debate this and arrive at the adjustments needed in the drivers to improve the forecast. In an ideal world, management does not need to ask questions in meetings, as they already have the answers.

Box 4: Enterprise analytics enables two-way flow of insights

Of interest to note is not whether the East regional manager has done his homework and has the right answers. The real point here is that management does not have the ability to arrive at this answer on its own, independently and with a single version of the truth serving all the sources of questions.

If all this information is available in an enterprise predictive analytics dashboard system meant for management, then the following courses of action could take place.

1. Management is informed (using the dashboard) that East region will miss profit targets.
2. Management drills down in the enterprise dashboard in real time in the meeting to identify which flights within East region are projected to come below their profit targets.
3. Management, VP of sales, and the East region head together look at the enterprise dashboard and understand the details driving the results. They learn that two flights are coming below their margin targets. They would further understand that these two flights are being impacted by low loads driving down the expected margins in the next two months.
4. Further, the enterprise optimization of the drivers of profits has already been run, and it would recommend a price drop of 10 percent to counter the competition scenario to maximize profit margins in the coming two months.
5. All of the above information is coming from the enterprise dashboards fed by Analytics 3.0 capabilities with 100 percent governance.

We hope by understanding the above process description, the reader is able to see the power of enterprise analytics and the process changes needed in running management meetings. It is clear that such an enterprise dashboard system using predictive analytics shows management drivers and results. It further recommends a course of action to optimize the results.

> We would emphasize that democratizing insights up and down the hierarchy has an extremely beneficial organizational benefit—that of shared leadership. Management meetings should eventually morph into opportunities of shared leadership between analysts, data scientists, knowledge workers, and layers of management. Single version of insights, reproducible in real time by anyone in this hierarchy and in any meeting forum—is the best vehicle for democratizing decision-making.

Today the gap between the knowledge worker and senior management is so wide that the concept of shared leadership fails and falls by the wayside. Peter Drucker wrote in the 1960s that "we do not know how to manage the knowledge worker so that he wants to contribute and perform. But we do know that he must be managed quite differently." This is still relevant and true.

7.4 INSTITUTION OF GOVERNANCE IN ENTERPRISE ANALYTICS

Given the dynamic environment of execution, it becomes critical to monitor leading indicators continuously. Most airlines are not able to have a read on leading indicators, which requires good predictive analytics. It requires the CEO and her team to play a major role in organizing people, processes, and systems for advanced predictive analytics. Once these are in place, they must be instituted to work well and keep improving. Governance of the predictive analytics systems is critical to improve execution. In this section we explore the critical role of governance for analytics.

7.4.1 THE ANALYTICS GOVERNANCE PROCESS

Governance is the oversight needed to ensure that execution delivers on strategy. We start at the top priority of the commercial organization—profit margins. Therefore, the first step in the governance process is to make sure that strategies and execution are directed at maximizing profits. Once this first step is done, everything the organization models and delivers should also aim to maximize profits. The idea to institute analytics governance is to drive execution and results. So we believe the process of governance should undergo a significant transformation at most airlines to enable this. It starts with using the advanced analytics system to drive every meeting, be it the CCO's council or any other review team. All information and insights (see next section) should come from the advanced analytics system. Within the system, predictive models and pre-scriptive models are executing continuously, piping results to the commercial team via dynamic dashboards. Commercial operational systems like the RM system, NP system, and sales systems will continue to be used by the commercial department. The advanced analytics based governance process ensures that results are always being reviewed each week, month, and quarter in meetings (or on demand anytime they are needed).

It is critical that the governance process does not impede operations. The results of operations are continuously in review through the decision support provided by these advanced analytics systems. This is the main purpose of the governance process - to review frequently and to take corrective action at the earliest opportunity to avoid gaps emerging between strategy and execution.

Advanced analytics introduces a significant number of models that serve the entire commercial department in optimizing profits. The models provide critical outputs which are enterprise insights to drive coordinated actions. In the absence of advanced analytics today, these models are embedded deep in Excel spreadsheets. Each manager is not only managing people and driving metrics critical for the business, but owning and manipulating numerous Excel spreadsheets that are driving decisions. Our experience suggests that very few of these models within the Excels go into the formal enterprise review process. These models are acting on data that have not been authenticated as the process does not call for authentications. Now this last point is very important. Most steps in the commercial decision making process do not enforce any governance rigor and it shows in poor execution.

The governance process should ensure that 100 percent of the data and the models used in advanced analytics are authenticated. This may not be easy to pull off at most airlines since Excel spreadsheets and the data embedded in them are virtually everywhere in the commercial department. Advanced analytics would require the process to move all data and model execution into enterprise systems and away from Excel spreadsheets. Authenticating the data and models is a journey, and if it takes time to get there, airline commercial leaders should make the case and get it done.

7.4.2   ROLE OF MANAGEMENT IN ANALYTICS GOVERNANCE

Figure 18: C-suite governance of analytics

Figure 18 shows analytics governance oversight provided by management. At the core of this is the CEO and the C-suite. They will define the main metrics for the airline and the key drivers of these results. They define where, when, and how these metrics will be tracked, reviewed, and improved.

Once the CEO and the C-Suite have defined the metrics that will be at the center of all their management discussions, the Chief Analytics Officer (CAO) is tasked with the responsibility of delivering the capability for the CEO to run this agenda. The modern role of CAO is necessary for the advancement of analytics within the organization. The CAO would harmonize the systems, models, and data within enterprise analytics and legitimize them as part of the governance.

The CIO is a powerful stakeholder in deploying analytics governance. Together with the business leaders, the CIO sets the systems architecture that will deliver predictive analytics based decisions to the enterprise.

Metrics set and pursued by the CEO and his team are well known within most well-run airlines, but the focus and discipline needed to monitor these metrics is at the heart of the analytics governance process. The C-Suite meetings should be looking at these metrics from a 360-degree perspective—historical, forward looking, and across all the dimensions where profits are being generated. Whatever be the meetings, the agenda should center on these metrics—results and drivers of results across dimensions.

The point is very clear: the most important part of analytics governance is the CEO's team focusing on the main results and drivers. Each of the C-Suite leaders could take up this central agenda with his or her team, ensuring governance top to bottom.

7.4.3 QUANTIFICATION

We end this section on governance with the following question. What is the need and benefit of having quantified analytics? This seems to be the central question we should answer as we institute governance for analytics and establish the ROI for the analytics investment.

We take an example to answer this. The VP of marketing at a global airline is considering approving a $5 million spend over 3 months to boost loyalty. The idea is to ask what is the ROI on the $5 million spend. To start, we would need to estimate the incremental revenues we can expect from this spend. Today's analytics within the marketing departments of most airlines would not be able to support such a quantification.

A more common and perhaps easier to quantify case would be the actions being taken by the sales teams. The idea is to ask, what is the ROI on the tactical promotional spend for increasing revenues on weak flights? To get to this quantification, we would have to estimate the incremental bookings and revenues these promotions would generate. Again, as much as this appears straightforward, there are no systems that can, in a verifiable way, quantify this.

Can RM systems predict the impact of pricing actions in a quantifiable and verifiable way? RM systems forecast using exponential smoothing, and these use past results, not future drivers to forecast. Airlines that have implemented pricing systems (different from inventory control RM systems) may be able to quantify, to some extent, impact of pricing actions. Whether they can do this quantification in all the dimensions where pricing actions are taken is up for discussion. We have not seen systems in action that can do this the way management would like to see the results.

So through the above examples, we can see that no systems can quantify in a verifiable way the revenue and profit impacts of most marketing, sales, and pricing actions. This is the clear gap that must be addressed in the advanced analytics governance agenda.

The main work of the CAO then is to ensure the advanced analytics systems quantify and verify the impact of marketing, pricing, sales and network levers in driving revenues and profits. Further the CAO must ensure that the data and models are bona fide. If the organization is in pursuit of the single version of insights every time there is a meeting or a decision to be made, then it is imperative that advanced analytics are bona fide and the results are quantified and verifiable.

7.5   TAKEAWAYS

- Execution takes place in microsegments of dynamic competition while strategy takes place in more static environments. This is a key reason why there is usually a gap at most airlines between expected and actual results.
- Today's state of analytics does not allow for most of the commercial functions to be able to track this gap in real time and correct course.
- To address this would be a top priority for airline managements worldwide. It would require a business process reengineering of the commercial function. Specifically, the reengineering should be focused on the following aspects:
  - o Development of enterprise analytics capabilities in the commercial function
  - o Development of enterprise insights to guide the strategy and execution process
  - o Institution of governance for enterprise analytics
- Advanced Enterprise Analytics is a paradigm-shifting capability that can enable airlines to execute better and deliver better results. Predictive and prescriptive analytics based on Big Data provide the best possible navigation in the dynamic and volatile execution environment.
- Real-time insights generated from the advanced analytics capability are communicated down and up the hierarchy of the commercial department. This enables the whole department to be united in pursuit of the common metrics and minimize execution risk.
- The C-Suite and the new function of Chief Analytics Officer work in concert and lead the governance process. They implement the advanced analytics capability and they use insights top down in all meeting forums to guide the teams to superior execution.

Eight

Dashboards Science

If you change the way you look at things, the things you look at will change.

—Anonymous

Dashboards are the main navigation tool available to the entire management team to stay aligned and progress toward meeting targets. While they are critical parts of management systems, and processes, we believe the power of dashboards in bringing together teams is not well understood. There are many reasons for this, but one of the big ones is that—like analytics itself—dashboard science has largely been delegated to the IT department as a BI project in most of the airlines. It is not something the CEO and his immediate team have embraced and passionately driven. We have found a very strong correlation between management involvement in developing a strong set of dashboards and management execution.

8.1 THE PROBLEM WITH TODAY'S DASHBOARDS AND ENTERPRISE INFORMATION SYSTEMS

There has been enormous interest and attention paid to management information systems, reports, and dashboards in the last twenty years. Most airlines have multiple BI projects at various levels—C-suite, senior management, middle managers, and analysts. These projects have one goal: to keep the decision-makers informed of the drivers and results so that the right discussions take place and the right decisions are made.

If we observe the way most airline managements operate today, we can draw several inferences about the gaps that exist in the goals of these information systems and reality.

Gaps observed:

1. From executives' meetings to lower-level meetings, historical reports serve as the available tool for making decisions about the future, underserving the needs of the executives.

2. These historical reports are not incisive to show the effect of decisions in shaping results. It's critical to note that today's reports do not have built-in predictive analytics that could show results in different scenarios.

3. Meetings are not supported by flexible reports and dashboards that allow for various future scenarios. Ad-hoc what if analytics are missing in the information systems today and they are the central need of management decision making.

4. Most meetings are run on data sourced from excels and localized sources. The data and models are not bona fide in all instances and in all meetings where decisions are taken. This calls into question the governance around decision processes, which we have highlighted before as inadequate.

We realize that despite significant interest shown over decades in getting the right information reports and systems, airline managements are still looking for the right solutions to help their decision-making objectives in meetings. We are at a unique point in the evolution of analytics and business intelligence, giving us the opportunity to address these gaps in the airline industry.

8.2 PRINCIPLES OF EFFECTIVE DASHBOARDS

Based on the above inferences, we present some key findings about dashboards that if followed become a critical part of analytics architecture:

1. *Dashboards should be intuitive as users are very busy.* Today's dashboards are excessively heavy and scattered. In an effort to allow the user to see most of the moving parts, the designers usually come up with a non-intuitive look and feel. It is critical for dashboards to communicate easily and effectively what the user most wants to track.

2. *Dashboards should motivate and drive action.* Results shown through gamification of the execution process is eagerly lapped up and is also motivating. Most organizations devote time, energy, and resources to motivating staff and driving up performance. Devoting dashboard design efforts to motivate staff is increasingly effective to drive positive change.

3. *Dashboards should be fueled by enterprise analytics, not excel spreadsheets.* As alluded to in chapter 3, most dashboards are sourced and made from data in Excel spreadsheets. This is at the core of why single version of the truth is elusive in most airlines and indeed most organizations.

4. *Dashboards should be effortless to use, to keep the user interested.* We have seen many versions of dashboards that are sent out as fat and laborious Excel reports making users navigate around to find insights. With new SaaS technologies in place, it becomes critical for most applications (including dashboards) to be available from the web browser. Dashboards should be intuitive, and simple, displaying the most critical information to the user without significant effort.

5. *Dashboards should focus on the end results—profits—at all levels in the organization.* This last main principle is the most important one. Nothing is more important than focus in dashboards. As we stated in chapter 2, the single most effective way to ensure coordinated commercial execution is to get the whole management team focused on the main metric. And that main metric is profits. Dashboards at all levels should show profits and profit drivers as the main focus relevant to that level.

In Box 5 we show an example of a company that is taking dashboard science to a different level. It encapsulates many of the principles we have talked about above.

Procter & Gamble: Advanced Presentation of Insights to Decision-Makers

Cincinnati based P&G is a global giant in consumer goods and has been so for nearly two centuries now. This venerable company is also a very proactive user of analytics. P&G has been unique in understanding the power of presenting data and insights to decision makers across it global operations. Using visual analytics P&G has standardized decision cockpits on most of its desktops worldwide enabling "commonality" of insights rather than "creativity". P&G has even taken steps to create decision making spheres or rooms that are specially fitted for management to be on the same page worldwide and discuss all insights as one common team. Managers worldwide are seeing insights of where products stand in their markets, displayed on heat maps. While innovative in the creative aspect, the main purpose Is not to dazzle the managers, but to help them understand quickly what's going on in the business to decide what to do about it. It's about getting beyond the what and moving to the why and the how. And it's not just the visuals that are common and standardized, but the information itself. Managers don't spend all their time comparing data, but agreeing how best to devise ways to address these problems. It's the creativity that is exercised on those fronts that really drives the success of P&G's managers.

Source: Harvard Business Review, April 2013

Box 5: P&G Advanced analytics dashboard example

8.3 DESIGN OF COMMERCIAL DASHBOARDS FOR AIRLINES

We build on the previous section and dive into dashboard design here. The dashboards that management see must be designed with an absolute focus on the key metrics that drive results. We believe most of the other metrics that are presented take away this focus. There are two main metrics that should be discussed at every enterprise or departmental meeting:

1. Performance Results
2. Performance Drivers

Before we get down to results and drivers that are best shown in the dashboards for airline commercial departments, we focus first on ensuring all functions are on the same page - multidimensional focus on key metrics.

8.3.1   PERFORMANCE RESULTS DASHBOARDS

Dimensions are the way we see the result - bookings or revenue or profits. For example, the sales department is focused on channels driving sales (not revenues). Similarly, marketing is focused on customer segments driving revenues. RM is focused on flights and routes driving revenues while NP is focused on flow traffic driving revenues.

The innovative dashboard design we show in Figure 19 can harmonize these differences in perspectives. It illustrates how such a dashboard might look for a particular dimension. It has a gamification based look and feel. Every dimension has the same focus – profit. Sub dimensions have the same focus – profit and they are shown along lanes. The result of the whole dimension is summarized at the bottom. Each lane shows profit target performance of the sub-dimension and the position on the lane reflects achievement forecast for the period being shown on the graph. It's all forward looking using predictive modeling.

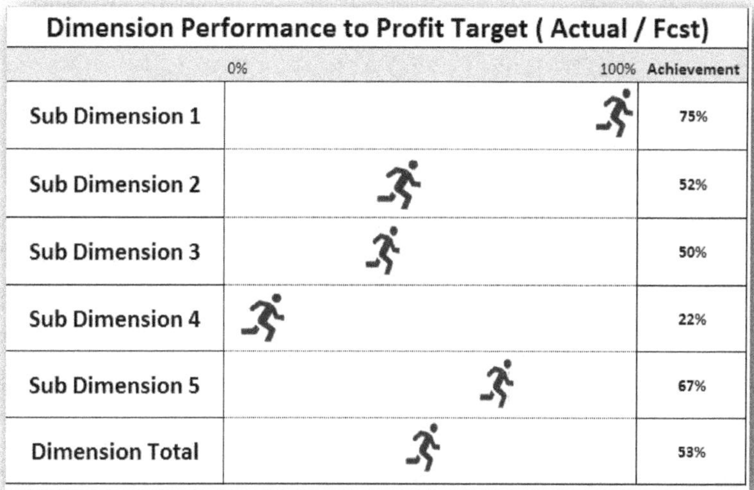

Dimension Performance to Profit Target (Actual / Fcst)		
	0% 100%	Achievement
Sub Dimension 1		75%
Sub Dimension 2		52%
Sub Dimension 3		50%
Sub Dimension 4		22%
Sub Dimension 5		67%
Dimension Total		53%

Figure 19: Dimensional performance dashboards

We next turn to what is driving the performance along any dimension.

8.3.2 PERFORMANCE DRIVERS DASHBOARDS

Profits are shaped by the same set of drivers across all the dimensions. We refer to the profit margin diagram in Figure 12, introduced in chapter 5. Aggregated drivers such as yield, volume, RASK or CASK are critical to drive profits, but are not primary drivers. They are not controllable as they are usually the result of more granular drivers. Granular drivers include Price Premium, Cost of Sale, Sales promotions, distribution promotions, marketing actions and frequent flyer benefits among others. So dashboards should show the granular drivers along each dimension.

Driver dashboards should communicate current drivers and optimal driver positions. This allows the users to understand where they are and where they need to move to deliver better results. They should further allow the user to visualize scenarios as they move the drivers and generate varying results. This will be elaborated in the next section.

Figure 20 shows a template driver dashboard to go along with a dimensional performance dashboard shown in the previous section.

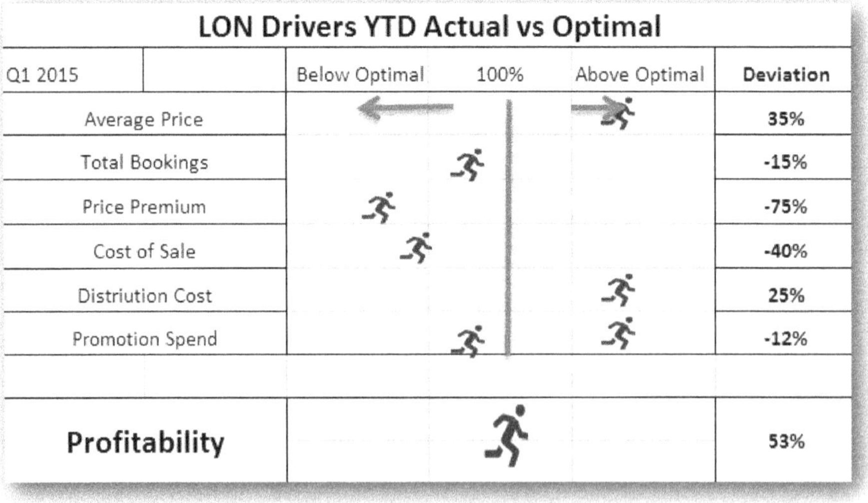

LON Drivers YTD Actual vs Optimal					
Q1 2015		Below Optimal	100%	Above Optimal	Deviation
Average Price					35%
Total Bookings					-15%
Price Premium					-75%
Cost of Sale					-40%
Distriution Cost					25%
Promotion Spend					-12%
Profitability					53%

Figure 20: Driver dashboards for dimensional microsegments

There are several critical things to note about this dashboard:

- The same driver dashboard and graphic can serve any dimension the user wishes to see (in this example, we show for LON POS, but it could be the same graph for any POS or any other dimension).
- The dashboard shows each driver in a lane calibrated around the center blue line which represents optimal value of the driver. The actual value being depicted is deviation from optimal.
- Optimal value of the driver is arrived at by critical predictive modeling based on Big Data.
- Drivers could be above optimal as well as below optimal. Both are undesirable as they would probably be delivering more profits if they were optimal (which is what the model is saying).
- The bottom lane represents the performance (profitability) of the dimension against its target.
- The dashboards are interactive and what-if enabled.
- The value in each lane can be moved closer to or further away from the optimal value, and the other corresponding values on the graph will change, including the profit in the bottom lane.

The manager using this driver dashboard is clearly informed where he is at present and where he needs to go with each driver in order to hit his performance target. This is a clear and simple focus on the main drivers of profitability across the dimensions he manages. In the next section, we focus on what more he can get out of such dashboards if they are really smart and futuristic.

8.4 SMART DASHBOARDS—DRILL DOWNS, SCENARIOS, AND WHAT-IFS

Modern dashboards serving advanced analytics are dynamic and use smart graphs. They are dynamic as they can depict scenarios based on changing inputs.

They have live models running behind the scenes. To start with they depict the below two scenarios:

1. Current state
2. Optimized future state

The dynamic dashboards could produce what-if scenarios of the future state with different combinations of driver values. That is the power of dynamic dashboards. In addition, these are actionable dashboards. They are actionable because they not only show past performance and gap to goals but also how levers that can close the gaps and drive higher profits. As mentioned above these dashboards are fed by real time advanced analytics models working continuously. This is one of the most important ingredients missing in today's static dashboards. This is the essence of dynamic dashboards. They not only get you the current and best options but also allow them to be customized and tracked later on—Analytics 3.0 in action.

8.4.1   ONE DIMENSION DRILL DOWN ON PROFITS

Using the commercial dashboard, the CEO is able to run meetings focusing on the number-one priority: profits of the company. This dashboard shows commercial margins. She could view it along any dimension using the concept of aggregations and drill downs.

For example, the CEO could choose the time dimension and get an aggregated view along all other dimensions. She could start at the highest level and navigate as described below:

1. Review the profit result of the last three years and forecast for coming year
2. Drill down and review results of the last four quarters
3. Review forecast for the next two quarters
4. Drill down on the time dimension and review the results of each month in the last quarter
5. Drill down on the time dimension further and review the results of each week in the last two months

6. Drill down on the time dimension and look at forecast of profits in the coming weeks for the next quarter

All this should be possible for an aggregation and drill down on one dimension such as the time dimension.

8.4.2   TWO DIMENSIONS DRILL DOWN ON PROFITS

Next let's look at how she could use two dimensions for the review:

1. Choose the time dimension and review the profit result of the last two quarters and the forecast for the next quarter
2. Choose point of sale as the other dimension to drill down. She could start by looking at profit forecast for the next quarter at the region-level POS
3. Move down from the region level to the country level forecast for the next quarter
4. Move down to a monthly forecast of profits at the country level
5. Move down to a monthly forecast of profits at the city level
6. Move down further to a monthly forecast of profits at the district level
7. Drill down to a weekly forecast of profits at the district level

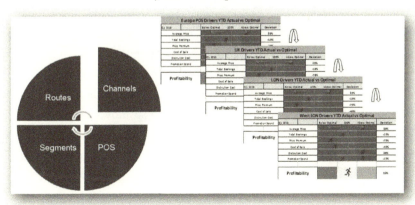

Figure 21: Multidimensional drill down in smart dashboards

Figure 21 shows how dimensional drill downs would work across two dimensions while keeping other dimensions at their highest level of aggregation. Let's focus on this particular graph we have displayed and explain the design characteristics. Here we show two things that are going on:

1. It shows the profit metrics as percent achievement to target. This is the focus of the metric.
2. It compares all the alternates at that level of aggregation and displays them as competing alternates. The concept is like that in a race. This is the gamification concept.

Most airlines set profit margin targets at the highest levels in the budgeting process. But our observation is that when we drill down across dimensions to even one level below the highest level, these targets disappear. This is strange and is a fact at most airlines. We believe it is perhaps the single biggest reason why most airlines are not consistently profitable. What gets measured gets delivered. The measurement has to happen at the places where results are getting shaped. And those are not in the boardrooms or the C-Suite. They are in the drill downs of the dashboards to the flights and POS and channels where bookings are taking place and profit margins are created.

In summary, what we have described are dashboards for Analytics 3.0—descriptive, predictive, and prescriptive. The opportunities are identified continuously and available at all management reviews. They are available for the C-suite, the VP level, the director level, the manager level, and the analyst level from all commercial functions. They show how the entire organization is delivering on commercial profit targets across this hierarchy, where the opportunities exist, and the levers that need to move to deliver on those opportunities. This is a powerful set of reviews, governance, and execution tools rolled into one application. This is a modern airline commercial-value-generation system.

8.5 TAKEAWAYS

- Most airlines are using outdated dashboards that are primarily backward-looking reports. These dashboards are not reliable to provide consistent insights across the commercial departments to drive the optimal decisions.
- The futuristic dashboards of Analytics 3.0 are powered by predictive analytics piping insights to management across the commercial functions. Analytical predictive models working on real-time Big Data are generating forward-looking insights in these futuristic dashboards.
- These dashboards follow the best design principles: they are intuitive, motivating, insightful, and certified. They aggregate and drill down among all the dimensions along which the key metrics and drivers need to be understood by management for decisions.
- The futuristic dashboards are used by all managers across the commercial departments for their decisions. It is the one source of the truth, delivering the same insights to all without need for interpretation. These dashboards are an integral part of the advanced analytics system of the airline.
- Commercial dashboards show results and drivers in the same look and feel across all dimensions and at all levels of the organization. This helps the commercial team to be always consistent in presenting and interpreting data. Results are presented with profit metrics and drivers. Aligning the whole commercial department on the same metric is critical for alignment.
- Smart graphs are a critical part of modern analytics dashboards. They are powered by real time predictive analytics and allow for drill downs, scenario modeling and dynamic what-if analytics. They should eventually eliminate excel spreadsheets which are at present the main analytics tools, albeit with limited data and modeling that is non-standard.
- Using these dashboards, managers can take decisions by literally being on the same page at any end of the process. Standard predictive models are run and presented with the same insights to all users, ensuring alignment. This single innovation in dashboard science is more important than any other in driving better commercial decisions.

Nine

Advanced RM Analytics

RM is the single most important technical development in transportation management since we entered the era of airline deregulation in 1979.

—*Robert Crandall*

In the next few chapters, we describe some of the applications of advanced analytics in the four core commercial department functions. We start with revenue management below.

9.1   REVENUE MANAGEMENT EVOLUTION AND CURRENT STATE

We get down into many details in this chapter on how advanced analytics can improve the RM function. We start by providing a recap of the main points from previous chapters on RM today.

Price is the most important driver of bookings and revenues. When the airline industry was deregulated in 1978, it set in motion a serious look at the pricing function to drive profits to airlines. The yield management (YM) function was invented to create the analytical horsepower to drive strategic and tactical pricing decisions. When YM was first introduced by some airlines in the mid-1980s, it became a significant source of competitive advantage for those airlines.

Early airlines that adopted YM reported an increase to their top line of 5–10 percent. Indeed, it has become common practice to think that RM can deliver that type of incremental gains consistently. Increasingly we have found that the competitive benefits of RM and pricing have been eroded over the last few years. We now observe that while not having an RM function can hurt an airline, it is not enough to deliver the type of incremental revenue consistently that early adopters experienced.

We are currently at the tail end of second generation RM systems (known as O&D or network RM systems which followed leg segment systems). We are seeing that as we get into the later stages of this product life cycle, there is a flattening out of the benefits of RM to the airlines that are adopting them.

In this same period, we find that RM function has been increasingly taking over the role of the main analytics team within the airline. If we have to restore the profitable contribution of deeply analytical functions to the airline, airlines must embrace some big changes to the way they practice analytics and put them to use. The revenue management and pricing departments are crucial to running analytics in most airlines today. We highlight the most important platform the RM systems offer for analytics:

- RM departments have systems that produce bookings forecasts on flights, which form the basis for many analytics around the airline.
- Pricing systems store details of pricing and promotions that drive bookings, information that is critical for analytics modeling.
- RM systems also are used for revenue forecasts using the forward bookings repository, which sits within it.

These core benefits from RM systems—booking forecasts, pricing and promotion levers, and revenue forecasts—bring the power this function wields over many discussions within commercial teams of today's airlines.

While we should keep the above in mind, we should also point out the constraints RM systems pose to the airlines:

- RM systems are operational systems more so than analytical systems. They are not designed or wired for analytics needed across the enterprise.

- Their data repositories are not designed to help answer analytical questions around sales channels, promotions, or specific customer segments.
- RM systems have not been reinvented for enterprise advanced analytics. Instead they have superficially changed to work with Big Data, without changing any of their core mathematical models.

To support true advanced analytics at enterprise level, departmental analytics need to undergo significant innovation. In the following sections we present advanced analytics that RM and pricing departments can and should run.

9.2 RM'S FIRST PILLAR - OVERBOOKING

In today's world of busy corporate travel, cancellation and changes to the bookings are common. Many network carriers today allow cancellations with a small penalty. For some special booking classes (typically high-yield classes and for business travelers) there is often no penalty on cancellations. Cancellations result in a reduction of revenue-producing bookings, and unless replaced with other revenue-producing bookings, revenue maximization would not be possible.

Overbooking is one of the pillars of the modern RM process allowing airlines to maximize revenues and yields on tight flights. Revenue integrity is the complementing process to ensure that tight flights are packed with the best revenue-producing bookings. Working in combination these two processes allow airlines to fill up the flights and eliminate spoilage. Current RM systems allow for overbooking at flight, cabin, and booking class levels.

We will see with an example how the current process works: A flight between A & B has 150 seat capacity. Airline does not currently practice overbooking. If demand exceeds 150 for a particular departure date, airline will not overbook per its policy. If there are cancellations or no shows, and no corresponding pickup of bookings, it could result in spoilage. With a change in policy allowing overbooking, and with a superior analytics to predict cancellations and no shows, the airline could entirely prevent spoilage. The more accurately it is able to do so, the more money it saves (or more revenue it generates).

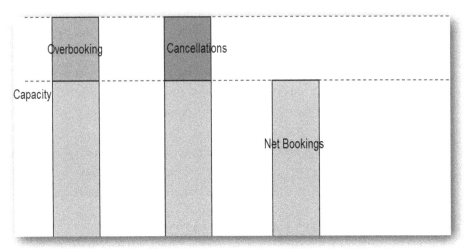

Figure 22: Overbooking protects wastage due to cancellations

To ensure minimum spoilage, airlines tend to overbook—say, up to 160 bookings in this case—if they are expecting about 10 cancellations. Figure 22 shows this in a simple way. The blue overbooking is done in order to counter the red cancellations and no shows. This is fine as long as the expectation of ten cancellations is accurate. However, if only nine cancellations come through by departure, and we have 151 passengers at the gate, then there will have to be one denied boarding on that flight. This causes customer dissatisfaction for the airline. Most airlines get this wrong occasionally and are willing to take on this small amount of brand value erosion, considering the advantages of saving thousands of spoiled seats had they not done so. So it becomes critical to improve forecast accuracy of cancellations, something which can be significantly improved with advanced analytics.

9.2.1   ADVANCED ANALYTICS FORECASTING OF CANCELLATIONS

Based on the above, it is clear that RM systems should be very accurate in predicting cancellations in order to maximize revenues and minimize the need for denied boarding.

Today's systems predict cancellations at the flight-booking class level. They do this by using time series techniques predominantly. This implies they would look at historical cancellations of flights and compute probabilities for future cancellations.

There are two problems in the approach taken here by the systems available today:

1. They focus on past timeline trends to project future cancellations. They are not able to model the impact of events on cancellations.
2. They are focused on cancellations by flight rather than cancellations by passenger type.

Using advanced analytics, explicitly modeling critical factors would improve the accuracy of expected cancellations. For this to happen, a causal forecasting predictive model would be more suitable than a time series model. In our experience, time-series-based forecasting systems are very useful in predicting such cancellation rates and accompanying loss of revenue. We need modern predictive analytics that can take Big Data inputs like customer details, weather, competitor moves or customer events to predict cancellations.

We show here how analytics can add customer characteristics to the mix of data used to predict cancellations. For example, we can associate a **cancellation index** with each customer or customer type. (simpler if we start with customer type and progressed to individual customers in due course). The index could range from zero to ten, and this is assigned based on historical cancellations by the customer type. The higher the index number, the better the quality of the index and the lower the probability of cancellation. The overall cancellation index calculated for each flight and its bookings is thus an indicator of cancellation probability. This could be an important driver in the predictive model for cancellations.

It is important to focus on the near-term window for cancellation predictive analytics—we would recommend doing it within ten days to departure. Otherwise the accuracy is impacted, and overbooking can deliver more volatile results. We have seen that RM-based overbooking decisions made earlier in the cycle could lead to reduced revenue opportunities.

Data is collected along the booking cycle, each departure is monitored, and the forecasting process is executed. The forecasting engine will identify the likely cancellations (using the cancellation index of the bookings as a key input) on each departure and compare that with the overbooking levels. It can then produce the type of graph shown in Figure 23 showing opportunities to improve on overbooking. These insights can be piped to the entire commercial department so that collectively the sales, RM and marketing functions can take actions.

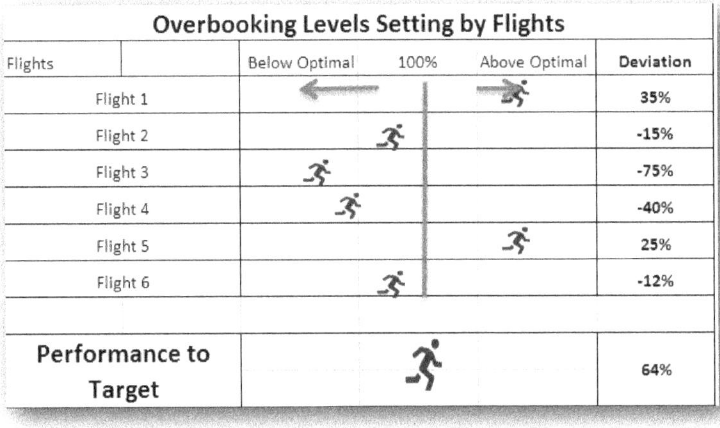

Overbooking Levels Setting by Flights						
Flights		Below Optimal	100%	Above Optimal	Deviation
Flight 1		←		→	35%
Flight 2					-15%
Flight 3					-75%
Flight 4					-40%
Flight 5					25%
Flight 6					-12%
Performance to Target					64%

Figure 23: Highlighting overbooking opportunities

The analyst or manager looking at this output would be able to arrive at decisions about which flight to focus on for improving the overbooking levels. For example, he can infer that overbooking levels are set too high for flight 1 by 35 percent, and we may have been too aggressive. Again he could infer that for flight 2, we have set overbooking levels too conservatively and that there could be more cancellations than we anticipate. Thus advanced analytics would provide guidance to the manager to improve on the overbooking levels in the system and deliver optimal revenues.

9.3 RM'S REVENUE PROTECTION TOOL - REVENUE INTEGRITY

The critical function of Revenue Integrity (RI) within RM is to ensure that non-revenue bookings are not displacing high yield revenue during peak demand. On these flights demand is much higher than supply, and the opportunity for higher yield is real. Bookings from earlier periods tend to have lower yields, but the target of revenue integrity will be nonrevenue bookings and obsolete bookings (canceled and still being maintained by the distribution channels). While it is important to ensure revenue protection throughout the booking cycle, revenue integrity is in play mainly during the last few days of a flight's booking, when demand quickly outstrips supply on high-demand flights.

The overbooking function has already set the amount of bookings above capacity that need to be taken to maximize revenues. On those flights where current forecast of bookings is higher than overbooking level set, there is a need to free up some inventory to maximize revenue. This becomes the main focus area of RI analytics. Applying this logic, daily analytics can be set up which will scan all the flights in the coming days to highlight opportunities for improving revenues on the flights. As this is multidimensional advanced analytics, the user can specify the channel dimensions for displaying the outputs. An example conceptual dashboard is shown in Figure 24.

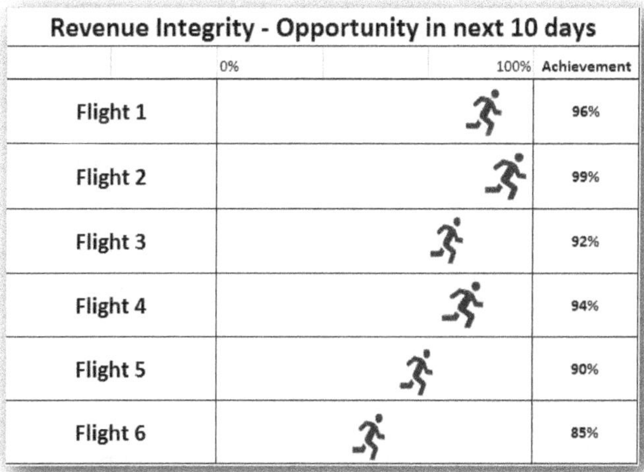

Revenue Integrity - Opportunity in next 10 days				
	0%		100%	Achievement
Flight 1				96%
Flight 2				99%
Flight 3				92%
Flight 4				94%
Flight 5				90%
Flight 6				85%

Figure 24: Highlighting Revenue Integrity opportunities

9.4 MULTIDIMENSIONAL DEMAND FORECASTING WITH ADVANCED ANALYTICS

Forecasting profits is one of the fundamental requirements for management to make good decisions and generate great results. Most airlines struggle with forecasting profits in multiple dimensions. While some have profit forecasting capabilities along flights, very few airlines have good profit forecasting at the enterprise level or across other commercial dimensions. This is because RM systems are wired to provide bookings and revenue forecasts along flight bookings classes. They are not flexible and cannot project forecasts by channels or POS or customer segments. This is a significant limiting factor and needs to be understood by the leaders of the airline as to why advanced analytics beyond RM systems are needed.

Sales systems - CRM (customer relationship management) and SFA (sales force automation) systems—do not include forecasting capabilities to be used by sales teams. They would depend on RM even for basic forecasting such as estimating lift from a sales promotion. Similarly, marketing departments do not have their own forecasting systems. Most network planning departments in airlines today do not have systems that support forecasting profits across multiple dimensions.

Given that today's forecasting systems are meant only for the RM department and cannot do basic things like those listed above, we present below what an advanced analytics forecasting system would contain:

- A forecasting system for the entire commercial department including RM, sales, marketing, and network planning
- A system that forecasts bookings, revenues, and profits, not just bookings
- A system that can provide what-if forecasting analytics with changing drivers

If a modern analytics system can deliver all the above, then it becomes a platfom on which the company can build a good analytics capability.

Advanced analytics greatly increases forecast accuracy. This is due to a shift in the whole DNA of the analytics - using state of the art predictive models working on Big Data inputs and running on machines designed to handle that data. These advantages were not available to RM forecasting systems a few years back. But even though they are now available, RM systems have not re-engineered enough to become enterprise advanced analytics systems.

In the context of multidimensional forecasting, common dimensions are route, POS, channel, customer segments, connecting traffic, and time. Each dimension can be set at any level. For example, POS could be set at country level for an international airline. Route could be all flights between country A and B (including multiple cities and flights). Channel could be set at retail. Time could be set at week level. Microsegments defined by the intersections of these dimensions are our units of forecasting. As we drill down along dimensions and into sub-dimensions, data is increasingly sparse to run the regressions. This is the trade-off that must be factored in while designing the forecasting dimensions and granularity.

We give below several dimensional forecasts that distinguish advanced analytics from existing RM forecasting capabilities.

Channel Forecasts: An airline may have five booking channels and may wish to forecast bookings at the channel level for the next twelve weeks. Today's RM systems cannot deliver this forecast. They do not forecast by channels, let alone sub channels and other interesting dimensional combinations. Using advanced analytics forecasting systems (as described above) channel managers across the airline are empowered to execute well. *They are provided accurate forecast of bookings for the main KPI they are driving.* They can drill across other dimensions and understand how their channel bookings change by routes or customer segments for instance. These are very interesting forecasts and done automatically by advanced analytics systems that are multidimensional capable.

POS Forecasts: An airline may have twenty POS organized geographically and may wish to forecast bookings at the POS level for the next twelve weeks. RM systems today cannot estimate POS forecasts as they are not wired to do so. That would need to be done in excel after exporting bookings from the RM system which record it by flight booking class. *With multidimensional advanced analytics capabilities, they would be able to produce forecasts and optimize by POS.* This will immediately empower every POS manager to take the best decisions for their KPIs and simultaneously for every route, channel and customer segment. This is how the multidimensional optimizer would work.

Customer Segment Forecast: An airline may have identified five broad customer segments and may wish to forecast bookings at the segment level for the next twelve weeks. Marketing managers are assigned to develop demand of these customer segments in the short, medium and long term. Yet no system in the commercial department today can provide forecasts of customer segments demand. RM systems today forecast demand by flight booking class, but not by customer segments. *Most marketing managers cannot translate booking classes to customer segments.* With multidimensional advanced analytics forecasting systems marketing managers are empowered to take the best decisions based on forecasts of the KPIs they are driving – customer segment demand.

The above is only a starting set for illustration of multidimensional forecasting using advanced analytics. There can be any combination of dimensions and levels that come together for forecasting. The more granular the forecasting needs, the greater is the data preparation required, ideally suited for the promise of Big Data analytics. Multidimensional granular forecasting can result in stunning insights to management.

9.5 DYNAMIC PRICING

At many airlines RM and pricing are two different functions. RM has the tactical function of inventory control while pricing has the strategic function of price setting. The price that we see on a booking is thus a combination of the price that was set and also the availability of inventory at this price point to be sold. This complexity of a two-part strategy of price setting and inventory control is often a cause for a lack of dynamic pricing abilities.

Today's RM and pricing systems focus more on operational effectiveness than decision effectiveness. Trading down from the principle of dynamic pricing stated above, they aggregate bookings into (price) fare buckets by implementing pricing within the inventory control based RM systems. Prices move in ranges of buckets that are opened and closed for sale by central RM analyst teams. This level of complexity has imposed significant latency in the pricing process. Price does not change with demand and customer willingness to pay as it should. The other significant barrier to dynamic pricing is the archaic distribution infrastructure centered around the GDS systems. They are built to show availability by fare classes and are not incentivized to change this anytime soon. They could be dynamic distributors by showing continuously changing fare points for the inventory, but significant system changes would be needed to do this. The present structure of incentives between travel agents and GDS companies is a big barrier for this innovation to happen[xiii].

The fundamental principle of dynamic pricing is that selling price can vary in a continuous way with demand changes. The more dynamic the selling price, the more the revenue capture. The higher revenue capture is possible as consumer surplus is reduced. This is the key to dynamic pricing.

Modern analytics are needed to support dynamic pricing. With the new systems and with Big Data analytical capability, airlines need to get smart about dynamic pricing and execute the decisions instantaneously as the opportunities arise. The pricing process should become nimble and so should the distribution process. Airlines should work with the GDS companies and change the way inventory pricing is handled to change dynamically with demand and customer type. It would take significant leadership from the airline CEOs to get this accomplished, but the profit opportunities far outweigh the collective inertia shown today. The next section describes a dynamic pricing analytics system that could drive decisions of the entire commercial department.

9.5.1   A DYNAMIC PRICING ANALYTICS SYSTEM

We present here a modern dynamic pricing analytics system that would address the issues cited above and position the airline for future scaling of capabilities:

- A dynamic pricing analytics system is meant for the entire commercial department—from the pricing analyst all the way up to the CEO. The system will answer pricing questions on any microsegment combination of dimensions across the airline's network. Typical dimensions could be flights, channels, POS, customer segments, connecting traffic, and time. The dimensions can be disaggregated and aggregated depending on the level of the user and their focus area resulting in large or small microsegments.
- The dynamic pricing analytics system will evaluate competitive pricing moves, demand and supply, and other marketing drivers to arrive at optimal price recommendation that will deliver this highest revenue

opportunity. It is a real dynamic pricing analytics system as it does not set price for any cluster of inventory, but recommends the best pricing change depending on current conditions.

- The system would be very simple to use and would not require data management or output design work by users. It would show the current and optimal values of pricing drivers in simple gamified user interfaces.
- The optimal price would be derived bottoms up from the transactions. These would be running daily on transactional Big Data and would present outputs on demand across the enterprise.

Let's see using an example below how the dynamic pricing system would be used.

An analyst responsible for pricing decisions of the web channel at an airline is considering pricing actions to deliver higher revenues from the channel. Today's RM systems cannot give him the required what-if analytics for his decisions. The analyst has been using the RM system for years, yet it does not provide decision-support analytics on how to change pricing to drive higher revenues. Obviously it cannot do dynamic pricing with changing conditions because it moves in blocks of inventory, which are sold at fixed prices.

With the new dynamic pricing system, the web pricing analyst can find answers to his questions. It would inform him of current price, price elasticity, and optimal price of this channel for every flight for the next month (or any other time window he chooses). He could query the system by changing the price point and get answers back about the revenue impact of these changes. These recommendations are optimized for the entire network across all selling channels and are the best possible answers for the web channel pricing change. Every colleague of the analyst, including the CEO, could query the system and get the same answer. He could change the time horizon and get the answers for the new time horizon as well. He could choose a different set of dimensions (not just flights) and see the optimal pricing for those dimension sets as well. The system allows him to be completely flexible in choosing any dimension set and see the price recommendation for those. This is the enterprise dynamic pricing system in action.

9.6   PRICE INVERSION

As bookings increase on a flight with each day, the price of new bookings increases steadily. This is the simple tenet of revenue management and pricing strategy. In reality, we find quite often that price inversion is taking place along multiple dimensions as a flight's bookings are picking up. As the bookings are building up, the yield is steadily going up until we find a sudden spurt in low-yield bookings due to a large sale (maybe across all channels) on this flight, inverting the .

Inversion can happen for multiple reasons, but the common thread is the way pricing, inventory control, and sales are disconnected. Pricing assumes that customer segments are clearly separated by fare fences, and that a higher price can be charged to inelastic customer segments (last-minute customers typically). RM inventory control allocates inventory in a progressive manner—which means closing lower-priced bookings progressively as bookings build up—leading to increasing yield till departure. Sales is usually agnostic to the specifics of inventory control on each flight but is generally aware that the earlier the bookings, the lower the price. They create demand in the market for near-term and far-out departures and leave it to the RM department to manage yield.

This loose connection between fare fences, inventory control, and the sales process can occasionally lead to pockets of lower-priced inventory during late stages of flight buildup. If this happens across all selling channels, we can see the type of drop in overall yield as described above. Our experience suggests that price inversion is a fairly common source of revenue leak. Significant revenue opportunity exists within most airlines to stop inversion on high-demand flights, driving up yield and revenues (1–2 percent annually in our estimate).

Today's RM systems are not able to provide predictive reports to spot price inversions ahead of time and avoid them. Advanced analytics can provide insights to the manager highlighting inversions and preventing revenue leak.

How do we spot inversion? They get this by looking at the price gradient of the bookings actually coming in. The airline revenue managers would come up with the business rules to spot a yield slowdown. For example, an airline could decide that two days of reducing average price and price gradient are enough to alert the managers of a possible inversion. So they would add additional variables in the enterprise analytics database to track and model pricing inversions.

9.7   CONNECTING TRAFFIC PRICING

Traffic that goes beyond a single flight and onto a second flight is called connecting traffic. Carriers can broadly be classified into two categories: Those that use network hubs to flow connecting traffic across these hubs are called network carriers. The rest (usually low-cost carriers) carry traffic point to point (P2P) without the use of hubs.

RM and network planning analysts are tasked with driving connecting traffic to maximize revenues for the full system. Today's RM systems come with leg-segment or O&D optimization capability. O&D systems are complex to set up and maintain. Their forecast accuracy is generally not as high as leg-segment systems. While O&D systems forecast and optimize inventory for local and connecting traffic, they offer very little support for advanced analytics of the connecting traffic.

While using RM systems, it is fairly complex to quantify the incremental yield, revenue, and profit increase, and hence the gains are not usually reported. Neither are the opportunities highlighted with proper quantification in the future space. This is again in line with the point we are making that today's RM systems are operational systems and not built for analytics. They do not capture the type of data needed to run complex analytics and report out incremental revenues and yields.

Network carriers rely on flow traffic to fill up individual flights that are connecting. The percentage of connecting traffic becomes a key determinant of profitability. Local traffic yield is usually higher than connecting traffic yield. This is logical, since if this were not the case, customer would end up buying two separate tickets. Given capacity constraints on a flight and therefore systems of flights, there is a natural economic effect of filling a flight with local and connecting traffic. While today's RM systems are able to recommend local and connecting traffic controls, they cannot quantify and present displacement economics. Modern advanced analytics are needed to help management understand the trade-offs and make decisions that maximize revenues. When demand is higher than capacity on a flight, there is a point where diminishing returns set in for incremental connecting bookings (due to their lower yield). The economics are positive till connecting traffic is filling the flight, but once it begins to displace local traffic—which is higher yielding—the economics start getting negative.

The challenge in practice is to arrive at this exact trade-off point for every connection in the system every day. Current systems without multidimensional forecasting and optimization capabilities do not get this quite right all the time as their forecasting is not always accurate. Neither are they wired to evaluate tradeoff in local and connecting traffic. That is usually left to the analyst to figure out. These gaps in accuracy of the tradeoff analyses result in loss of revenue, which can add up over time.

> Our estimation is that about 1–2 percent of total revenue of the airline can be lost due to suboptimal trade-off between local and connecting traffic across the network.

Advanced analytics can be used to arrive at the optimal answer to this trade-off for each flight in the future. The analytics forecast local and connecting traffic on each flight and identify the optimal mix across the network. They highlight the gap between the current forecast of revenues and the optimal revenues with the best trade-offs. They further identify the movement needed in each demand lever to deliver the optimal mix.

We use a hypothetical example in Figure 25 to show how the predictive modeling would work. In this example the current breakdown of connecting bookings to local bookings is about 40 percent to 60 percent. This is forecast to currently produce about $ 100 million in the next quarter.

Using predictive analytics, the system is able to forecast that if we lowered connecting traffic to 35 percent and increased local traffic to 65 percent with a 1 percent reduction in overall load factor, the new revenues would be higher, at 103 percent.

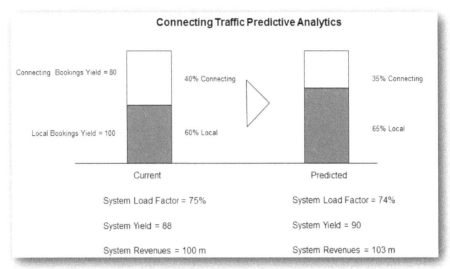

Figure 25: Connecting traffic optimization with advanced analytics

The above is just the starting point of the connecting traffic advanced analytics. Using predictive analytics, management can further drill down and understand the particular flight departures where connecting traffic can be reduced to execute and achieve the above modeled result.

9.8   NETWORK AND INTERLINE PRICING

Let's now focus on analytics for connecting traffic pricing. Often, we see pricing deals offered on connecting routes at a price that is lower than the sum of underlying flights. That is normal, but fare construction is not always easy for airlines to implement (especially for Interline pricing).

We list below some critical issues network pricing managers face today:

1. Pricing is often a constructed fare for a connecting itinerary rather than a simple published price.
2. Fare construction can be complex for large network carriers and may introduce errors as they involve considerable systems and business rules to come together.

3. These errors may not be detected till a passenger requests such a fare as there is rarely a quality control unit within the pricing and RM departments.

4. Pricing is always benchmarked very carefully with competition, and as a result, network pricing may be deliberately illogical at times in pursuit of being competitive.

Pricing should reflect demand and supply but should also appear reasonable to customers. If they believe they prefer a direct flight, then they would be willing to pay more for that direct service rather than connecting. Direct flights sometimes show lower fares than connecting flights, which is probably not preferred by customers. If this is deliberately priced and published so by the pricing and revenue teams, it is right (though not intuitive to customers). Otherwise it is either wrongly designed by the pricing team or wrongly constructed as listed above.

Advanced analytics would show this potential anomaly to the pricing managers. Like all other analytics we are prescribing, it should be done through an enterprise paradigm—enterprise models running on enterprise databases. These analytics would show anomalies in the bookings in the past and, using predictive models, project out what would take place in the future. They can show both forward- and backward-looking quantification.

As an example, Figure 26 below shows network pricing opportunities routewise for a carrier. The managers looking at this on an ongoing basis would understand where to focus and what decisions to make. This could be of significant help in reducing network pricing anomalies and saving between 0.25 and 0.5 percent revenues for the airline.

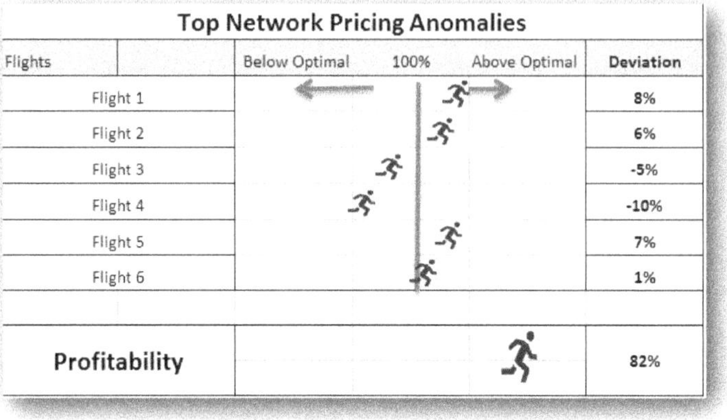

Top Network Pricing Anomalies						
Flights		Below Optimal	100%	Above Optimal	Deviation	
Flight 1					8%	
Flight 2					6%	
Flight 3					-5%	
Flight 4					-10%	
Flight 5					7%	
Flight 6					1%	
Profitability					82%	

Figure 26: Highlighting network pricing opportunities

As we pointed out above, some of these may be by design and some may be by error. It is the job of the pricing and commercial managers to review these dashboards periodically (recommended weekly) and take corrective actions.

Interline bookings are made on two partner airlines. One is selling the booking to the customer. The other is the partner airline on which part of the journey is completed. Interline pricing and alliances are done to increase sales reach to those customers and destinations where each airline is not flying. Interline arrangements can be through special pro-rate agreement (SPA), Code Share or Alliance structures.

SPAs are pricing arrangements between co-operating airlines to drive interline traffic. They are usually not considered deep co-operation and do not require ongoing marketing efforts to execute. A large airline could have hundreds of these globally with many other airlines and it allows for accepting and pricing interline traffic. Codeshares are marketing agreements that go beyond pricing. They allow for airlines to execute joint marketing activities like earning and burning miles in the FFP program, baggage benefits and convenience, sharing of lounges among others. Alliances are large arrangements among groups of airlines and tend to be very marketing oriented. They bring about broad sharing of benefits the chief among them codeshare and branding benefits. If executed well, these partnerships can deliver 5–10 percent incremental sales.

To execute interlining, partner airlines have inventory sharing and revenue sharing arrangements. Revenue sharing arrangements are usually based on miles flown or the proportion of the pricing offered on the legs individually. It is acceptable for airlines to charge a premium to the partner airline for sharing the inventory. This is usually on a reciprocal basis and is generally a win-win as it is incremental sales to both carriers.

Commercial arrangements notwithstanding, there are plenty of opportunities for interline pricing to improve the revenues and profits at many airlines. To start with, sometimes interline bookings have higher yield than average bookings on the flight, and other times lower yield. We can assume that higher yield was driven by good pricing and revenue management policies. But when yields of interline bookings are lower than flight average, then perhaps there are opportunities for better yield management. Advanced analytics can look into interline bookings and yields based on past data and current bookings and highlight opportunities for increased yields and revenues. This again is based on enterprise analytics running on enterprise databases.

Figure 27 shows the type of analytics output that could be shown to the interline pricing manager.

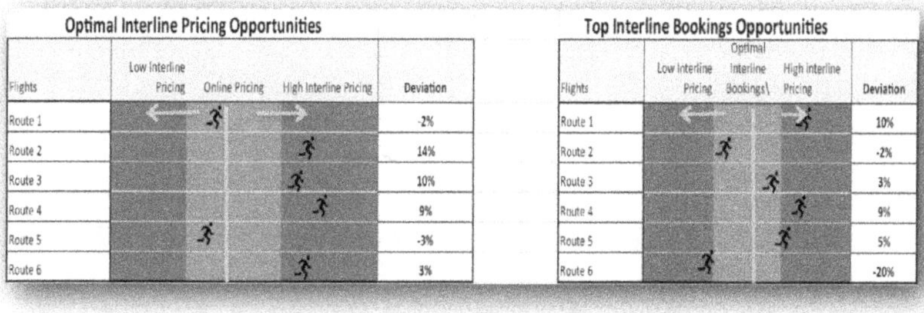

Figure 27: Highlighting interline pricing opportunities

9.9   TAKEAWAYS

- RM systems are operational systems more so than analytical systems. Hence they are not designed or wired to help the company with all types of analytics needed across the enterprise. Their data repositories are not designed to help answer analytical questions around sales channels, promotions, or specific customer segments.

- RM systems have not been reinvented to make them drivers of Big Data analytics across the enterprise. Instead they have superficially changed to work with Big Data, without changing any of their core mathematical models.

- Using Multidimensional Predictive Analytics, RM systems can fundamentally improve forecasting all around. They deliver a forecasting system for the entire commercial department including RM, sales, marketing, and network planning. A system that forecasts bookings, revenues, and profits, not just bookings. A system that can provide what-if forecasting analytics with changing drivers

- Advanced Analytics based RM systems can forecast bookings and cancellations more accurately on all dimensions, which sets up the platform for better Overbooking and Revenue Integrity.

- Advanced analytics based RM systems can identify dynamic pricing opportunities in the multidimensional space. Pricing inversions can be spotted and highlighted as they are forming, saving significant revenue dilution.

- Advanced analytics based RM systems can dynamically evaluate and optimize tradeoffs in connecting vs local traffic and online vs interline traffic.

- The above notwithstanding, a complete advanced analytics based RM system highlights every opportunity through dynamic dashboards to the entire commercial department. This takes RM enterprise wide from being a functional process.

Ten

Advanced Sales Analytics

Science is the progress that takes us from confusion to understanding.

—*Anonymous*

Sales (along with RM) is the other core revenue-generating engine of airlines. Sales teams are concerned primarily with developing and shifting short-term demand in the marketplace for the airline. Typically, sales departments are headquartered centrally but extensively distributed across the entire footprint of sales activity. They receive reports from headquarters and have limited analytics capabilities. Sales meetings are not run with rigor needed to deliver above expectations in every market. Sales performance metrics are testimony at most airlines that overhaul is needed to drive better results.

In this section we will describe how advanced enterprise analytics can be used to transform the sales function of a modern airline and boost performance. We focus on sales channels, sales force, sales agencies and sales promotions to illustrate ways advanced analytics can significantly improve performance. Let's explore each one of them in turn to see how advanced analytics can help drive the best performance.

10.1   CHANNEL ECONOMICS ANALYTICS

Channel economics is a critical analytics exercise within the sales department that we see missing in most airlines. Associated with each booking is a revenue and cost, driving margin. The total bookings in any channel produce all revenues, costs and margins for the channel. We mathematically show this simple reality below:

Margins of Channel = (Revenues of bookings – Cost of bookings)

Each booking is making a contribution to the overall channel margins. Hence it is critical for the commercial head to do two things using analytics:

1. Increase the margin of each booking and therefore the margin of the low-margin channels
2. Increase share of higher-margin bookings

As the sum of all channels represents the entire business, the goal of the commercial head must be to extract the highest margins from all the channels. This is the main focus of channel economics.

Using advanced analytics, channel managers could have a system that provides the below advantages:

- It gives a complete snapshot of each channel's yield and cost profitability.
- It shows contribution share of each channel to overall margins.
- It projects historical channel shares onto a future time period using predictive analytics.
- System evaluates continuously the overall revenues/yields/costs and margins, and this should be published to the entire sales and revenue organization.
- The head of sales can review the channel mix frequently as needed and take actions to improve sales of underperforming channels.

Channels are worked continuously by the sales teams in selling bookings around the clock. To make the channel economics analytics work, the airline would capture the revenue and costs of every booking in the advanced analytics database. Revenue recording is relatively straightforward, with interline and connecting traffic bookings making it a little more complex. The sourcing and rules are straightforward and, once coded into the system, can be expected to be accurate and correct. Bookings commercial costs are a different issue altogether. Many cost items are not tied directly to producing bookings. Many are allocations, and it is difficult to trace most of them in real time as bookings come in. But that is both the challenge and the opportunity.

Let's look at promotion costs for a booking. It is not very simple to allocate a promotion cost to each booking, as easy as it sounds. The main issue is that promotions are run across time and across the channel, and bookings follow. The promotion spend can be in bulk across the bookings, which is indirect cost attributed to each new booking. This becomes an allocated promotion cost. Or the promotion spend can be for each booking, in which case it becomes a direct cost. Either way we must find a method to assign a promotion cost to the booking and answer a couple of basic questions: What is the total promotion spend? What are the bookings generated by the promotion? The total promotion spend is divided by the bookings to arrive at promotion cost per booking.

GDS distribution cost is easier to track as it is priced per booking and by GDS type and booking type. There is usually no allocation required, and it is computed more easily than other costs. It can be computed from the commercials in the GDS contracts.

Frequent Flyer Program(FFP) and marketing cost should be allocated to the booking, something most airlines are not able to do. Total FFP spend for the given period must be divided by FFP bookings to get to FFP cost per booking. What most airlines do is a faulty way of allocating FFP cost by burn rather than earn of FFP miles. We believe it is the earn that must take the cost allocation, not the burn. In other words, we must impose a sales tax rather than a consumption tax.

Other costs such as credit card costs, special technology costs, and processing costs associated with the mode of distribution are also allocated to the booking.

Hypothetically, if a booking is made through an American Express card, then the airline may need to pick up about 2 percent of the total cost of the booking. If booked through Visa, the cost could be 1 percent. If the same booking is made by paying cash, then the incremental cost is zero. The airline may not be able to pass on these costs to the agents or customers in all cases and thus they become a cost of booking.

Once the revenue and cost allocations are applied to each booking, running channel economics analytics becomes relatively straightforward. If this is not done right (as is the case in most airlines) then channel development decisions are not right at the aggregate level as they are not built from ground up using the right cost and revenue allocations.

10.2   AGENCY ANALYTICS

Indirect sales through agents still account for the majority of bookings at network airlines. Managing this channel is critical to sales productivity and margin maximization. Out of this, a big portion comes from the higher-yielding sales from corporate travel management companies (TMC).

TMCs and retail agents do not own inventory, but they own the customer relationships. Their main value proposition is the value-added services they provide to the corporate travelers. They understand the needs of the travelers and make it easy for the corporates to manage travel, which is not their main focus. In turn they are compensated on a transactional as well as a retainer basis. They are paid by the airlines, the corporates who are traveling, and the GDS companies, who carry the content for making the booking. It is a complex set of relationships between the various parties involved. While airlines consider the GDS and travel agencies as a necessary cost of sale, they are always looking to reduce this cost as it can be substantial. In turn, though, they get a bankable business with a very healthy yield.

For most network carriers, corporate traffic is the most important customer segment, offering a staple high-yield business around the year. The largest of airlines compete with each other to carry this traffic and have departments dedicated to developing this channel. Let's describe this channel a bit before talking about the analytics for the channel.

Corporate bookings, like other bookings, can come from direct channel as well as from the agency channel. But increasingly, agency bookings are moving toward direct channel bookings. Airlines are making significant efforts to get bookings moved from OTAs and traditional agencies onto their websites, and it is happening. But in the corporate segment, the agencies are very powerful and entrenched. This is because corporates treat travel as an important part of their business that needs to be "managed" like any other aspect of their business. They would not like to encumber their traveling employees, who are on a different mission, to manage travel. Hence they still continue to rely on TMCs.

Airlines like to pay agencies only for the bookings made by the agencies and not for the self-bookings made by the traveler on their own. Some pay on the full set of bookings. Some pay on only corporate-coded bookings. Some pay higher amounts on high yield and business-class bookings. So there are a lot of variations and business rules in what payouts will be made to the agency by the airlines. So the economics of the agency depend on a lot of factors and not just on the overall volume from the channel. It requires careful coding of the rules to know the precise cost of these bookings. Most airlines do not even approach the cost of bookings in their optimization pursuit. But for those that want to use advanced analytics to optimize margins, the rewards can be very good.

With advanced analytics agency managers would have a system that provides the below advantages:

- It gives a complete snapshot of each agency's cost and yield and therefore profitability.
- It provides the head of agency channel sales the right percentage of contribution each agency needs to make.
- It allows for frequent (anytime) measurement of sales by agency.
- It allows for evaluating periodically the agency channel for optimization.
- It highlights the drivers of underperformance in lagging agencies.

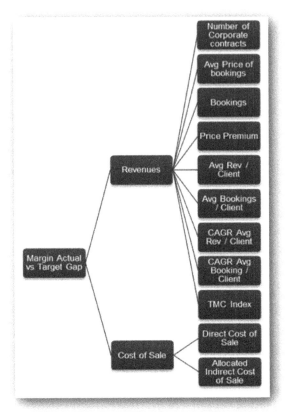

Figure 28: Agency performance drivers

Figure 28 shows drivers of agency performance. As we have continuously mentioned in this book, the output variable is margins (not sales or revenues). This is driven simultaneously by revenues and costs of getting those bookings, which in turn are driven by a number of second-level drivers of profits.

Agencies are worked continuously by the sales teams in selling bookings around the clock. To make the agency channel analytics work, we must be able to capture the revenue and costs of every booking. This feeds from the transactions and is aggregated to agency level bottom up. All in real time, on the go, with zero latency. That is way of advanced analytics.

10.3   SALES FORCE ANALYTICS

The performance of a modern network airline depends quite significantly on the effectiveness of its sales force. While many modern LCCs derive an overwhelming majority of their sales from their web channels, most airlines still have sizeable sales forces both for retail and corporate sales. Despite all the strategies that sales leadership can put into place, execution is critical to ensure the right results. Execution in turn is critically dependent on the effectiveness of the sales force. Ultimately it is the execution of your teams that is the differentiator with the competition, as most strategies can eventually be copied and neutralized.

Airlines looking to develop the right strategies for their sales team typically go through rigorous analyses, often with the help of consultants. We list some of the analyses we have seen in such efforts:

- Sales force production analyses: Top-down analyses of revenue/salesperson
- Sales force pipeline conversion analyses: Historical average size of the corporate acquisition pipeline; historical conversion rate of pipeline prospects to clients
- Sales force contract performance analyses: Contract compliance in terms of achievement to target
- Sales force to territory mapping analysis: Number of salespersons in the territory; percent penetration of clients/agents in the territory
- Sales organization structure analysis: Ratio of manager to salespersons in each territory

These are all hindsight business intelligence. Once the airline is able to identify these metrics, they appear to have some insights, but in reality these are intermediary insights not leading to results directly.

Let us distill this and showcase the way modern advanced analytics should work. The sales head needs to know how the team has performed, but more importantly needs to know the focus areas to improve the most. As shown above, most airlines that pay attention to sales force performance do so with hindsight business intelligence, not predictive, forward-looking insights. It is more critical for the managers to understand actions that should be taken to improve future performance rather than just rewarding past performance (which is also important, just not sufficient). Predictive analytics should be used throughout the performance planning, target setting, and tracking processes. Here the sales head gets a clear understanding of where his POS as a whole are against their targets and also where they are forecast to be. The predictive model should be able to forecast the sales achievement for each POS. This should be dynamic, and the time range can be day, week, month, quarter, or even the rest of the year. Sales teams are energized by healthy and positive competition. Gamification enabled analytics dashboards are a critical part of advanced analytics, delivering insights in the most motivating way and driving better execution.

In summary, the predictive analytics should be focused on insights that deliver results:

- Target setting: Opportunity size and capabilities should be modeled correctly when setting targets.
- Output simplicity: The output metrics are very simple. It is percentage of sales target forecast to be achieved. The sales target should be revenue margin, which is something we are consistently recommending throughout this book. The output also shows driver metrics that are driving the results.

Figure 29 shows the salesforce drivers that move profit margins. The salesforce drivers are worked continuously by managers in selling bookings around the clock. Running advanced forecasting models using these drivers shows how profit margins are shaping up. This allows for insights produced by advanced analytics that are not possible to see using traditional BI.

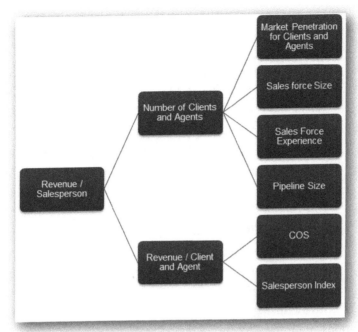

Figure 29: Sales force performance drivers

10.4 SALES PROMOTIONS ANALYTICS

Corporate deals are focused on high-yielding corporate traffic, offering them year around annual contracts. They are strategic, aimed at giving the airline a sustained competitive advantage by winning the loyalty of corporate traffic. Promotions are more tactical in nature and generally aimed to boost load factors. They are not sustainable over longer periods as they tend to bring down the market price (competitors usually match them) and the yield for the airline unlike corporate deals which attract high yield traffic.

Promotions need to be analyzed for the net effect they bring to the airline—incremental positive margin bookings.

In applying these analytics, it is critical to get both parts right:

1. The promotion's incremental revenues (from incremental bookings)
2. The promotion's incremental cost of sale

The difference between 1 and 2 is the net impact of the promotion's lift to the bottom line.

It is important to get the cost of sale per booking right in order to model the promotions analytics right. The ETL process would quantify the right cost to load into the bookings for the promotions. Usually this is modeled out before the business case for the promotion is built and the promotion run. If the promotion is approved and is running, then we need to update the correct cost per booking. The more accurately we allocate these COS spend to bookings, the better our results would be when we forecast and optimize analyses for profit margins.

We share below highlights of the way promotion analytics work:

- They give a complete snapshot of each promotion's profitability—revenue lift and cost of promotion
- Predictive intelligence provides the head of sales a snapshot of all promotions and impact for future period profits.
- Each day promotions should be evaluated, and overall incremental margins should be published to the entire sales and revenue organization.
- The head of sales should review the promotions mix and take needed actions to improve sales of underperforming promotions.

Promotions are run continuously by the sales teams in selling bookings around the clock. To make the promotions analytics work, we must be able to capture the regular and incremental revenue and costs of every booking in a database ready for advanced analytics modeling. Let's make it clear that it takes collection of data that shows regular and incremental demand. This is the crux of promotions modeling. It's about incremental revenue and cost recording that is driving incremental demand.

Enterprise analytics optimizes profit margin drivers across multiple dimensions. Sales promotions are one of the fundamental drivers along with price in the multidimensional space. Its effectiveness impacts the performance of the airline across this multidimensional space, but it is not the only force doing so. There are pull and push factors that drive performance optimization. Price, cost of sale, cost of distribution, and FFP programs being some of the other main drivers.

> Recording promotions data is not complex, but requires purpose and intent to do it right. We find that most IT departments and commercial teams are not able to record data meticulously and so cannot run these analytics effectively.

10.5 CUSTOMER ANALYTICS

Traditional airline customer segmentation classifies customers into the following broadly accepted segments: business travelers, leisure travelers, frequent flyers (who may be business or leisure travelers), group travelers, and special segments, such as students, elders, defense personnel, and so on.

Each of these segments may be classified further into sub-segments. For instance, business travelers could be classified into Monday–Friday travelers, same-day travelers, or one-way or return travelers. Frequent flyers could be classified into gold, silver, or bronze tiers depending on points accrued based on miles traveled with the airline. Leisure travelers could be classified into long-term, medium-term, and short-term booking travelers.

In today's airline systems, customer segments are based on the type of transaction and the booking class associated with the purchase. Customers are classified into a segment type based on the purchase type they have made for that particular booking. This is a significant drawback in the way airlines are understanding and leveraging customer segments today.

The relationship becomes transactional as the customers get classified according to the segments their booking falls under. This is significantly against the core marketing principle that customers belong to a segment based on their characteristics over a period of time rather than over the last transaction.

Customer Lifetime Value (CLV) based customer interactions lead to profitable growth of the customer base, while transaction-based interactions lead to suboptimal and even value-destroying growth of the customer base.

CLV can be calculated for individual customer as well as corporate clients. Once calculated and updated, the CLV database can be used in directing critical sales and marketing actions. B2C marketing efforts need to focus on creating long-term value in addition to getting to the short-term results. It would result in greater loyalty of the customers and also an increase in value to the company. It's a win-win situation, and analytics should drive these actions.

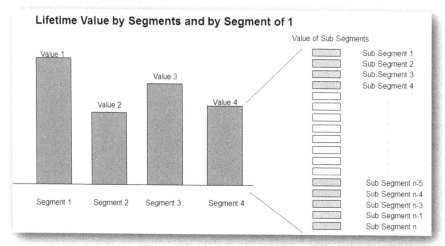

Figure 30: Customer Lifetime Value segments and sub-segments

Figure 30 shows corporate clients and customers classified into segments based on the lifetime value they represent. Each segment represents clients and customers of similar value grouped together for focused sales and marketing efforts. This is a modern and futuristic way of customer segmentation.

With such a segmentation approach, commercial departments can direct actions based on expected value of segments. All sales and marketing activities should be undertaken with a long-term view. They focus on getting more out of the best customers in the long run as represented by the lifetime value, and benefit in the long run. For example, if the sales team is looking to increase sales in a region, with this approach it has a pecking order of targeting clients based on value to the airline. Within the high value clients, there is a pecking order of FFP customers. Here the value based segmentation in the FFP database should be leveraged to identify the best customers and best clients to target the sales efforts.

CLV is not the only criteria for choosing clients to target sales and marketing activities. Client presence by route could vary and client response to promotions and activities could vary as well.

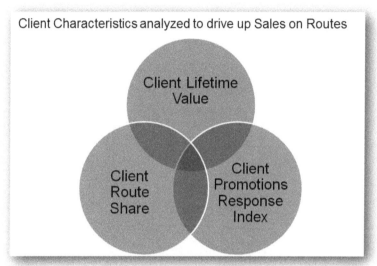

Figure 31: Drivers of client promotions

Figure 31 shows three drivers that would overlap when identifying clients to target for sales and marketing activities for specific routes. One of them is what we focused on in this section, the CLV. The other drivers are client size (and route share) and client responsiveness to promotions. The advanced analytics driving sales and marketing therefore would need to factor in all three drivers while arriving at optimal actions.

Multidimensional analytics should become part of the routine business decisions facing sales managers. They would use the advanced analytics database, which stores the inputs as well as outputs of (1) client lifetime value, (2) client route share, and (3) client promotions response index. Using a combination of the three, they could arrive at a composite index to rank clients for targeting the marketing activities.

10.6   RISK ANALYTICS

Today's airline systems do not have risk management tools to aid Commercial leadership teams. The only systematic analytics that exist are within RM systems used to monitor and manage flights. Other Commercial functions do not have visibility into RM tools anyway. Advanced analytics tools we describe here would contain multiple-level risk analytics built into them.

- First-level risk analytics: This is designed to show *known* risks in achievement to target. It looks back at past periods across dimensions and points to gaps where these risks exist, quantifying the size of risk. It uses descriptive analytics extensively to deliver this risk assessment. It helps management understand flights, sales regions, channels that have not met budgets on volumes, revenues and profit margins
- Second-level risk analytics: This is designed to show *emerging* risks in achievement to target. It is focused on the future period across dimensions and points to gaps where these risks are emerging, quantifying the size of risk. It uses predictive analytics modeling extensively to deliver this risk assessment. It helps management understand flights, sales regions, channels that are not likely to achieve budgets on volumes, revenues and profit margins
- Third-level risk analytics: This is designed to show *risk mitigation actions* to close the gaps in achievement to targets. It shows management the drivers of risks and what steps may be taken to reduce it. It uses optimization and prescriptive analytics modeling extensively to deliver recommendations.

Most airlines are barely able to cope with the first-level risk analytics. They do not have timely dashboards and reports that tell them where and how they are missing their targets. A primary reason for this is a poor level of analytics even during planning. They do not have well-defined targets along all the dimensions that they can track with sufficient granularity during the execution phase.

To get to the second and third levels of risk analytics involves getting to a platform for advanced analytics that gives them capabilities in predictive analytics and prescriptive analytics. This is an Analytics 3.0–level capability as we have referred to in section 2.3

Risk analytics is the domain between the commercial and finance departments. Finance typically sets the high-level strategic requirements across departments of delivering revenue above the total cost and thus return value to the shareholders. They spearhead the annual planning and budgeting process. This is a collaborative effort between all departments who input revenue and cost estimates.

During this collaborative process, the commercial department provides revenue and commercial cost inputs. All other departments provide cost inputs. This gets into the system (mostly an Excel-based system with significant human interventions) coordinated by finance, which runs multiple iterations and negotiations of the budgets.

The commercial head is constantly providing inputs to the CFO and CEO in management reviews on how the revenues and profits are tracking with respect to the planned budgets. The most central risk analytics discussion revolves around understanding short-term, medium-term and long-term revenue and profitability risk, and the steps management needs to take to mitigate them.

Advanced analytics are very much needed in quantifying these risks accurately and in a timely way, presenting them to management for the right decisions. There are three key aspects to how advanced analytics can help most airlines have a good risk management process:

1. Accuracy in planning and risk assessment
2. Timeliness of risk assessment
3. Easy presentation of the risks to management

Each one of these areas is very important, and today's airlines are not in a position to mitigate risk because they cannot consistently excel in each of these.

Advanced analytics using causal forecasting techniques can significantly increase planning and execution accuracy. The drill down on numbers that make up bookings along various dimensions can be assessed more carefully. Trends in drivers of bookings, revenues, and profits can be identified more clearly, enabling planning to be guided by predictive analytics rather than by gut-feel techniques. Inaccurate planning is one of the critical factors leading to poor risk management.

Advanced analytics can also significantly improve risk management by providing timely intelligence. Today's business intelligence takes a significant amount of effort to get to the right insights and information in most meeting settings, be it a C-Suite meeting, a Vice President meeting, or a manager meeting. Advanced analytics will correct all of these shortcomings. They present continuous updates in real time to all layers of management. Airlines using advanced analytics supported with a real governance (see section 7.4 on analytics governance) on performance can quickly assess where performance gaps are showing and therefore where the risks are, and can make decisions to minimize those.

With smart dashboards that are updated with real time modeling and improved BI presentation capabilities, advanced analytics cascade information instantaneously across the enterprise. Every meeting forum has the full access to every single risk in revenues and profits across any dimension. This is one of the key tenets of enterprise risk management. With its enterprise-level database, models, and dashboards, modern advanced-analytics-based BI democratizes insights and pipes them to all forums that may need them. This is the holy grail of perfect BI and perfect risk management.

10.7 TAKEAWAYS

- Sales teams are distributed across the airlines' footprint of sales and depend on headquarters based reports to help them execute. For the most part they receive standard backward looking reports on performance and forward looking bookings reports. Any analytics is done in excel environment. Given this environment of distributed teams, lack of strong analytics systems and basic reports to work from, modern sales teams need a significant boost of analytics to outperform competition.

- While RM has their own system for operational analytics, Sales teams do not have any such system. Advanced analytics systems deliver a significant advantage to this crucial department which along with RM is tasked with delivering the commercial revenue.

- Advanced analytics can deliver a significant advantage by automating the modeling and decision support in several key sales processes such as channel management, agency management, sales force management and client management.

- Advanced analytics provides significant improvement in customer loyalty through predictive analytics techniques that take customer lifetime value creation as central to customer decisions. This enables the entire commercial organization to make decisions that always increase the lifetime value of the customer base.

- These analytics can show the risks that are emerging in the future space and the actions needed to deliver optimal performance. Delivered through motivating and insightful gamification-based screens, such a system can elevate average teams to super performing sales teams.

Eleven

Advanced Analytics for the Travel Industry

More and more guests who would have booked at the front desk are in the parking lot booking on an app. The issue here is there are a lot of hotels playing the game of dropping rate on the last date and they're teaching customers to check the app before checking in.

—*MARK MORRISON, VP CORPORATE STRATEGY, HILTON WORLDWIDE*

Many of the main issues presented for airlines are valid for other sectors of the travel industry. Hotels, car rentals, cruise lines and rail companies face similar commercial issues. We focus on the hotel and car rental industries and showcase the issues in the context of advanced analytics.

11.1   ADVANCED ANALYTICS FOR THE HOTEL INDUSTRY—WHAT TO LOOK AT

The drivers of Hotel commercial margins are quite similar to that of the airline industry. Hotels have high fixed costs and perishable inventory that gets recycled every day to generate daily revenues. Airlines do this for every flight departure. They have similar distribution networks through global distribution systems and travel agencies. They have similar revenue management systems where inventory-control-based pricing is practiced to segment customers and extract maximum price. There is one structural difference that needs to be kept in mind when developing analytics for hotels: airlines tend to be centralized in their HQ for most of the commercial functions except sales. Hotels are decentralized in most of their commercial functions, including sales and RM.

Hotel margins—commonly measured as GOP—have been dwindling in the past several years. The declining margins are driven by lower unit revenue, higher fixed costs, and higher commercial (sales, marketing and distribution) costs. Sales and distribution costs in particular are taking a large toll on hotel margins. Hotel industry ROE to shareholders is only marginally better than airlines, at 5.7 percent compared to that of 2.5 for airlines[xiv].

In this scenario of very low margins and ROE, it becomes imperative for the commercial leaders in hotels to work in close coordination and deliver the highest RevPAR (Revenue per Available Room) and margins. Till recently, revenue management, which was invented in the airline industry, has been growing in importance within the hotel industry as a key function. But with the scenario depicted above—mainly after the Internet became a key channel and medium for demand—distribution and margin management have become equally critical as revenue maximization. Without an obsessive focus on margin management, hotels will become increasingly unprofitable as an industry, and several individual hotels and chains may go out of business as a result.

Therefore, we believe that CCOs must take up advanced analytics as a way of doing business and drive insights-based decisions every day and in every meeting.

11.1.1   THE RM DIFFERENCE IN AIRLINES AND HOTELS

One of the key differences we see in how most hotels run revenue management as opposed to the airline industry is the use of discounted bookings in filling up the inventory. The airline industry uses booking windows far more effectively and follows the principle of yield management more effectively. They close out low-yield bookings more rigorously and do not allow access to this inventory for any channel closer to departures. We have observed that most hotels will have

lower-yielding inventory available through the online channels (or other channels occasionally) late in the booking cycle. This hurts yields in the short run and revenue maximization in the long run as it establishes a belief in customers that cheaper rates may be available even close to arrival date at these hotels on select channels. Marketing and revenue functions must understand this long-term impact of undisciplined RM practices. While it may not be prevalent uniformly in all hotels and among all channels, the hotels' GMs will be well served by using advanced analytics to identify and plug these gaps where they exist, making the difference between profit and loss.

To be able to identify these trends, the decentralized RM function (at property level) should be understood well. RM is usually decentralized in most hotel chains, allowing the revenue manager at the hotel to set price controls. This practice is followed in large part due to the ownership and franchise model of the hotel industry. The ownership is often local and not central, and therefore levers of profitability such as revenue and occupancy are monitored and owned by each hotel as a franchisee. The operations are more in sync with the larger chain, but the specifics of the profitability depend a lot on each hotel's dynamics and management. This has historically been the case leading to processes and systems supporting local pricing controls. Revenue managers tend to follow local competitive pressures and define a "comp-set," which is a set of hotels in the vicinity of their hotel that is the primary competitive landscape. Most pricing decisions are taken with respect to how price-competitive the hotel needs to be compared to the comp-set rather than with company-wide pricing strategy.

11.1.2 UNDERSTANDING THE TOTAL SPEND AND NOT JUST ROOM SPEND

Unlike in the airline industry, a hotel stay is significantly longer and offers opportunities of increased revenues post booking. These can be categorized as ancillary revenues but are rarely tracked well and connected back to customers and clients in understanding their total spend. Most RM systems that support pricing to maximize room revenues have yet to start incorporating total revenues into the equation. Room revenues make up between 60 percent and 80 percent at most

163

large and medium hotels that offer food and beverage (F&B), meeting and banqueting services. Maximizing room revenues and not including the other 20–40 percent is missing a big piece of the revenue pie. But it goes beyond revenue as we have been stressing so far. Costs and profit margins are associated with each booking as well. The complete picture of maximization of commercial margins should therefore address room as well as ancillary revenue.

Let's illustrate this using a simple example of how pricing decisions taken only on RM's room-based capabilities can be insufficient for margin maximization. For example, offering a discount of $200 on a week's stay to a guest who spends $400 at the hotel on F&B during the week may be a more profitable decision than losing that guest to a competitor. For the hotel RM manager to make this decision, some analytics have to be in place. First he must recognize the customer uniquely for individualized pricing to be offered (CRM analytics). Then he must be able to assess that this customer is likely to spend $400 on a week's stay (predictive analytics). Third he must arrive at the financial decision of what is the incremental value of that $400 F&B spend in terms of profit margin (fully allocated predictive analytics). If as a result of all these analytics, he finds that offering a $200 discount to retain that customer on this request is more profitable, he can take it. RM systems of today definitely cannot deliver this type of deep and cross sell analytics.

This type of total spend analysis and discounting at POS based on customer lifetime value is not easily available to most hotels. Investing in rich capabilities of advanced analytics will result in recognizing this type of opportunity every time and can make the difference between profit and loss in the long run.

11.1.3 UNDERSTANDING TRUE CHANNEL ECONOMICS DRIVERS

Understanding your channels' profit economics is critical to optimizing margins and profits. With increasing power of intermediaries, most hotels are limiting the GDS channel and moving toward increasing Brand.com share. This may be the desired way to maximize channels economics, but the reality could be quite different for different chains and properties within chains. The GDS channel accounts for about 15 percent on average and produces the highest margins other than the Brand.com channel. It has higher margins than call centers, OTAs, search engines and affiliates on the Internet, and any other channel. Some hotels understand this and drive their economics according to the reality of their data. But most of the hotels don't understand this, and there is a common approach among all of them to move bookings out of GDS and into the Brand.com.

So how does a hotel chain go about understanding the profits of channels and make the right decisions of maximizing margins? They would need to track margins along each booking. Bookings data need to be augmented with attribution that brings the cost elements into clear view at the most granular levels. Every booking is happening across multiple dimensions (channel, POS, room type, property, and time period) and it is important to allocate the right variable cost associated with that booking for sales, marketing, and distribution costs. Once this difficult exercise is done, it must be maintained each day with the most relevant information for accuracy of the allocated costs. If this degree of work is done once upfront and maintained daily, then it sets forth the foundation for proper channel economics.

Channel economics reflects the ongoing evolution of demand and supply equilibrium playing out in each channel and across channels. The demand is being impacted by the cost of sale and cost of distribution in that channel. There are intermediaries, and they require to be paid to deliver the bookings for those channels. But equally the demand is being impacted by price in that channel. This is true of any microcosm in which economics forces of supply and demand play out. We need to understand that demand drivers are not just the push elements represented by cost of sale and cost of distribution. Demand is very much driven by price within each channel. So a complete channel economics analysis includes the pull element of price and the push elements of COS and COD. The hotel would be well served to project this dynamic for the short term and the way it would evolve in the medium to long term. This could shape its short-term tactical approach and long-term strategic approach. We have observed that the more closely the short-term approach is aligned with the long-term approach, the better the economics play out for the hotel or any other company in any industry. It's just too expensive to change tactics into a different strategy over the course of the medium term.

11.1.4   COMP-SET ANALYSIS—IT CAN BE MISLEADING, LEADING TO WRONG DECISIONS

As explained above in section 10.1.1, hotels have a distinct local competitive nature even while being part of larger chains. Hotels within a segment compete on price and product for the local demand. So they are very careful to match price and product as much as possible on their comp-set to keep market share.

Comp-set analysis is important, but can be misleading because the analytics needed to understand it comprehensively is missing. Third-party data such as the reports from Travelclick provide snapshots of market share and price comparison among the comp-set. It is important to note these are snapshots at best. They present the picture as of today. These vendors may be able to provide deeper analyses if required, but their products available to hotels remain snapshots. Revenue managers should do a lot more to augment this snapshot data before making tactical and strategic pricing decisions.

Short-term RevPAR decisions to gain bookings and boost occupancy can have long-term impact on profitability. It is important for all the hotels in the comp-set to realize that long-term demand can be profitable and stimulated using appropriate push and pull levers, but lowering the price to increase daily occupancy can have detrimental long-term impacts. Comp-set analyses can cause a lot of noise. Advanced analytics are needed to separate the signal from the noise.

11.1.5   MARGINS ARE CRITICAL—REVPAR IS NOT A SUFFICIENT METRIC TO OPTIMIZE

One of the major themes of this book has been that margins are critical to understand and optimize at the microsegment level and not just at the income statement level. They cannot be optimized at the income statement level except during the planning stage, which is an optimization game on paper. The real game is played out during the execution stage—which is virtually all the time—in bookings at the microsegment bookings level. Each day bookings are being made in these microsegments, and the bookings deliver revenue at margins. What determines margins on the income statement are the margins of these bookings at the microsegment levels—hence our theme that margins are the metric to optimize during execution to deliver what has been planned. This is one of the critical gaps in commercial systems today. They can either focus on revenue or cost, but not simultaneously on margins. Optimization should be done by focusing on both simultaneously.

Hotel bookings so far are optimized to deliver the best RevPAR, which is a revenue metric. RevPAR derives from room rate and room occupancy. But this constitutes only 75–80 percent of total revenues in the hotel industry. It leaves out two major parts that make up the difference between profit and loss. It leaves out revenue from banquets, F&B, and meeting and events. It also leaves out the cost of acquiring this business and the commercial sales, distribution, and marketing costs. So with ancillary revenues and commercial costs not being factored for optimization, we find that profits are not actually maximized in this pursuit of RevPAR.

11.2   TMC

Travel management companies (TMCs) provide booking and travel management solutions to corporate travelers worldwide. They serve corporate clients on the one hand and the vendors of travel products—airlines, hotels, car rental companies—on the other. While typically they used to be part of the umbrella of travel agencies, their total-solution approach to a focused segment of the travelers—the business traveler—has earned them the name of travel management company, as they are "managing" the travel needs and travel functions of their clients.

They have powerful IT investments for sourcing and distributing content from suppliers to agents worldwide. These are mainly operational infrastructure, but they have also made strides in reporting infrastructure. However, they do not have state-of-the-art Big Data–based predictive analytics of the kind we have been describing in this book so far. The same can be said for the hundreds of smaller corporate travel agencies in every country. Big Data predictive analytics is not commonly found or invested in by the TMCs.

11.2.1   TMC REVENUE MODEL IS BASED ON SERVICE FEES AND MANAGEMENT FEES

TMCs do not own inventories of flights, hotels, and cars that are used by their corporate clients. As a result, they do not directly price these products and services. They facilitate the sales of these products and services and in turn they are compensated both by the vendors and the clients. In addition, they are also compensated by the powerful GDS companies that carry the content on behalf of the vendors. The GDS companies provide the shelf space while the TMCs provide the storefront where the sales happen. In applying analytics to the TMC landscape, therefore, we must understand their revenue model quite well and identify how revenue and margin maximization can be effected through advanced analytics.

Clients contract with TMCs to manage their travel and deliver the best value at the lowest cost of travel. Clients may have travel requirements to various parts of the world, and they would not be able to develop strong supplier relations in all these parts to get the best deals. This is primarily because they are not in the "travel" business, but travel is an activity they need to perform to conduct their main business. Hence they rely on TMCs to whom they "outsource" the procurement and fulfilment functions that take care of their travel needs. They negotiate contracts with TMCs through formal Request for Proposal (RFP) processes and select a particular TMC after rounds of negotiations on capabilities and procurement rates leading to the best possible deals. A client would usually select a single TMC for all its global travel needs if the TMC is able to deliver globally. Otherwise the client may choose to go with multiple TMCs, arranging to be serviced by the best TMC for each region for both service capability and procurement capability. Clients usually compensate TMCs with service fees and management fees, which can have a fixed component and a variable component. The variable component is usually larger and is driven by the number of transactions.

Suppliers contract with TMCs to drive higher volumes (traffic) through their airlines and hotels when clients travel. Usually clients have a few key suppliers empaneled to allow customers a limited choice of carriers and hotels. This is best practice as it allows for best "preferred" procurement rates and is easier to manage as well. One of the key negotiations between suppliers and TMCs is on the volumes expected to be driven to them and compensation for incremental volumes beyond the "expected" threshold. The contracts are usually implemented in a slab structure with higher payouts for higher slabs.

The TMC revenue models therefore are tied to the transactions or traffic driven for all their clients by the TMC across various suppliers. By increasing the number of clients and getting the best supplier and client contracts, the TMC is able to maximize their revenue streams.

11.2.2   TMC GROWTH ENGINE—NEW CLIENT ACQUISITION

As in any B2B business, new client acquisition is the growth engine for TMCs as well. The sales function in a TMC is operating in a competitive environment and winning in the marketplace through service differentiation and better pricing. Client acquisition is driven by many aspects of sales effectiveness, including value proposition to clients, capabilities of sales teams, and brand power of the

TMCs—all of which result in a pipeline of clients that are converted over time, resulting in top-line growth of traffic. This top-line growth is critical for TMC execution. TMC sales teams should pursue a balance of responding to Request for Proposal (RFP) and self-initiated client base in the pipeline. RFP is the way for clients to request TMCs to bid for the business of managing their travel. Most large clients globally have already contracted with one or more TMCs at this time. These can be multiyear contracts and, at the end of the contract period, can come up for renewal or new RFP. When there is a new RFP request, the TMC will respond and compete for that business. Non RFP client base is developed by the initiative of the sales team in identifying clients who are likely prospects.

Pipeline strength is a critical driver of sales success in B2B environments. Pipeline analysis should include portfolio distribution, number in pipeline, conversion rate, and probability, leading to a valuation of the pipeline. All of these can have second-level drivers such as sales force capabilities, cost of sales, training, and compensation. Pipeline valuation should be forecast for a future period and measured against targets. As seen in this description, this involves quite a bit of analytics, and most TMCs are not able to do this today. Instead they rely on the expertise of their sales managers to deliver client acquisitions without significant analytics. Modern predictive analytics based on pipeline analytics can be a significant improvement in delivering on sales targets.

11.2.3   TMC EXECUTION—OPERATIONS EXCELLENCE

TMCs are operations-centric businesses where delivering the perfect experience for the traveler including flawless booking and fulfilment are of prime importance. Clients pay travel management and transaction fees to the TMCs primarily for the efficiency and thoroughness of service. This in turn requires the booking agents to have high efficiency and knowledge of the travel parameters, including options for searching and delivering the desired trip at the lowest cost. They must understand the traveler's needs, match it with the suppliers, and deliver it with the least bit of difficulty. The ways in which the trip details are communicated, retrieved, and made available to the traveler are dramatically changing these days, so the technology solution is a critical part of the value proposition.

TMCs focus on several key metrics to drive operations excellence. Productivity, client loyalty index, cost per travel agent, and revenue per agent, are among the common ones. There are financial drivers as well, such as error rates, conversion rate, and communications per booking. These are in turn drivers of the main bookings. There are no standard analytics tools available to drive operations performance management. Every manager uses his homegrown tool to model and increase the results from these metrics.

As in an airline or a hotel, there are several multidirectional dependencies of the operations team with other functions. Operational excellence results in increased revenues for the company driving both client and supplier revenues, which are handled by other functions. Similarly, the sales function has downstream effects on all other functions.

It gets very complicated to model the interrelated effects of each function on all the others. Hence we do not see any analytics solutions in this space so far. The main analytics solutions for the TMC space are developed in-house using Excel spreadsheets. Using a standard system across the functions integrating the data, modeling, forecasting, and optimization across these functions is the best way to drive advanced analytics at TMCs.

11.2.4 TMC EXECUTION—HR EXCELLENCE

Supporting the TMC's core business model of delivering the perfect trip to the business travelers is the Human Resources (HR) team. The HR angle of performance is surprisingly not understood in quantifiable ways to model business results more accurately. We find this is true at a TMC as much as it is true at an airline or hotel or any other product and service industry except for the professional services industry. Presently, there is no system that can understand the efforts and impact of individuals and reflect it in a model used for forecasting and optimization. While there are systems usable by HR departments to meet their requirements, the point being emphasized here is the quantification of human resource inputs into forecasting and optimization modeling for the business.

Typical HR metrics at a TMC could include the following:

- Performance rating of staff
- Training needs and training levels
- Productivity of staff
- Revenue/staff, cost/staff, margin/staff

Even with just the above, we can begin to contrast the current systems with what advanced analytics can deliver. Current HR systems and processes may be linked to SAP like enterprise operational systems or be run on standalone Excel spreadsheets. Either way, they have weak system support for HR decisions during execution. As an example, TMCs see continuous performance variations in how their teams are executing—in the dynamic environment of client demand and supplier changes of inventory and pricing—to deliver the perfect trip experience. These variations could be caused by a variety of reasons, including employee skill sets inadequacy, training inadequacy, excessive volume of work, or a lack of employee engagement. The continuous stream of bookings data contains rich information that needs to be understood to make sense of the noise and the signal. Understanding this requires a system that in real time is monitoring patterns and extracting the signals. Today's HR systems and processes cannot handle this type of volume and variety of information and get the details into coherent signals. Advanced predictive analytics systems are designed to help TMCs execute their HR function to identify the drivers of performance in real time and deliver the best results.

11.3 TAKEAWAYS

- Hotel industry advanced analytics is similar to that in the airline industry. Using advanced analytics, the hotel industry can address some shortcomings of RM-driven analytics so far.

- RM in the hotel industry should move beyond room-based revenues. They must include a complete revenue perspective that brings food-and-banqueting revenues and meetings-and-conventions revenues into the optimization paradigm along with room revenues.

- The hotel industry should further understand the changing dynamic of distribution costs, which are threatening their margins. Traditional TMC and GDS channels are decreasing, while OTA and Brand.com are increasing their share. This is not always the best result or the best strategy. Yields, costs, and margins should be fully factored in, and optimizing commercial margins (GOP) rather than revenues is the way forward.

- Travel management companies are critical intermediaries in the airline and travel market. They play an important role for profitability of airlines and hotels as they control clients who are the bread and butter of the corporate travel segment.

- Advanced analytics can bring together the different departments of the TMC like sales, supplier management, operations, client management, and HR. Today most of these analytics are being executed in silos as in the airline and hotel industries. It is imperative for the CEOs of this industry to develop advanced analytics systems to optimize profit margins and not just pass along the burden to the source of inventory they help optimize.

Twelve

Appendix

In the next few pages, we present further collection of useful pages for the CEO to guide the airline in the advanced analytics journey. They are under these topics:

- The Advanced Analytics Playbook
- Advanced RM Analytics Use Case – Regional Airline RM Department
- Advanced Sales Analytics Use Case – Global Airline Sales Department
- Multidimensional Advanced Analytics – A primer
- Chapter Summary Collection – Handy reference for implementing the Playbook

12.1   THE ADVANCED ANALYTICS PLAYBOOK

We present first the playbook for implementing advanced analytics. This is the summary form of the description in section 6.4. A CEO can use this as a 12 step strategic project and get the competitive advantage she craves.

Today's airline CEOs and management teams are very busy trying to deliver the best results. CIOs and their IT teams are very busy driving multiple projects and managing large budgets running the information needs of the airline. In this continuous cycle of tight schedules and pressure to deliver the best results, long-term strategic investment in scalable analytics capability for the future is not an assured strategy. We present the steps needed to deliver a paradigm shift in optimization:

1. Define advanced enterprise analytics as a key profit-generating lever.
2. Define the incremental profit range expected from enterprise analytics.
3. Institute a governance body and objectives for enterprise analytics, tying financial results to the enterprise analytics paradigm shift.
4. Define common profit margin results and drivers across all the commercial departments.
5. Task the chief commercial officer with delivering this system and driving the governance results expected from advanced analytics.
6. Institute a chief analytics officer to work with the analytics governance team and drive the enterprise analytics as a fast, dependable, and accurate system.
7. Identify a system architecture that will deliver the layers of an advanced analytics solution
8. Procure an advanced analytics system—which uses artificial intelligence and machine learning—from a vendor dedicated to the airline industry and its particular needs.
9. Redesign your business process to bring together all commercial functions —sales, revenue management, marketing, and network —and to optimize levers at the enterprise level across these departments.

10. Require the advanced analytics system to provide predictive, prescriptive, and scenario analytics.
11. Using this comprehensive system, every commercial decision will have an analytics-based recommendation for optimizing profits.
12. Benchmark and review results from the system and tie them to company profits. Publish the results in the annual report of the company.

12.2   ADVANCED RM ANALYTICS USE CASE – REGIONAL AIRLINE RM DEPARTMENT

Figure 32 below is a summary of the project we delivered for a regional airline in advanced analytics. We demonstrate the need and importance of advanced analytics in the RM department through this example. Chapter 2 describes this example in detail and provides the context fully.

Regional Airline Use Case - Revenue Management Advanced Analytics Project				
Projects	Redefinitions / Data Organization	Measurement	Calibration	Results
Forecast Enrichment	Seasons were not correctly defined	RM system was not measuring forecast accuracy	Map bookings to correct seasons	We are able to increase Forecast accuracy by 10%
	Each Flight Analyst defined seasonality for his flight	We put in place analytics to measure it at multiple levels	Calibrate forecast parameters	
	No automated tool availability for this so significant rework was needed	The analytics measure forecasty accuracy at Class, Flight, Route , Systems levels	Improve the forecast	
	Clean up of historical bookings		Iterate on calibration and improvement	
Revenue Integrity	Bookings data used for RI analytics needed significant cleaning up	Measure RI system performance	Calibrate system performance	Improve revenues by 1 %
	Cleaned up Unticketd Bookings which were obfuscating the analytics	Estimate Revenue loss by flight	Put in place fixes to system errors	Reduce GDS costs by 1%
	Cleaned up Non Revenue Bookings which were obfusctating the analytics	Identify RI system errors	Put in place new biz rules to clean out bookings	
Overbooking	Bookings data used for overbooking analytics needed significant cleaning up	Measure system performance	Fix parameters of overbooking system	Results
		Identify critical flights needing Overbooking		
	Cleaning up Unticketed Bookings		Iterate on calibration and improvement	Improve revenues by 1%
	Reduce Non Revenue Bookings	measure current overbooking		
Dynamic Pricing	RM systems do not have pricing data well organized for analytics	Measure Pricing Elasticity along all dimensions	Calibrate elasticity models along multiple dimensions	Results
		Identify pockets of elasticity and		
	Organize data for price elasticity analysis	inelasticity	Run multiple dynamic pricing pilot projects	2% lift in revenues
	clean up inversion and missing data		Improve dynamic pricing and scale up	
O&D Management	Airline did not have data organized by O&D	No O&D data meant no real analysis happening on flow traffic	Put in place O&D Pricing	Results
		Pricing and inventory control were sub	Put in place O&D Inventory Control reports	
	convert leg seg data to O&D data	optimal as a result	and support	1% lift in revenues
Bottom Line Impact of Advanced Analytics Project - Increase Revenues by 5% Profit Margin by 10%				

Figure 32: Advanced RM analytics - use case at a regional airline

12.3 ADVANCED SALES ANALYTICS USE CASE— GLOBAL AIRLINE SALES DEPARTMENT

Figure 33 is a summary of the project we delivered for a large global airline using advanced analytics. We demonstrate the need and importance of advanced analytics in the sales department through this example. Chapter 2 describes this example in detail and provides the context fully.

Large Global Airline Use Case - Sales Transformation Advanced Analytics Project				
Projects	**Redefinitions / Data Organization**	**Measurement**	**Calibration**	**Results**
Customer Segmentation & Channel Economics	Customer data was scattered across departments and systems	Customer metrics like Value, Profitability was missing for both B2B and B2C segments	Fine tuned the analytics to reveal economics of each segment within the channels	Clarity on value proposition and value delivered by each segment and channel
	No clear definitions and value propositions to main customer segments	We put in place data integration and measurement analytics for Direct and Agency Channels	We improved the measurement to allow the data to unveil the true value proposition to each segment	Results in better decisions around product , price and promotion offered to each segment, channel
	We brought data into one Sales Data Mart , cleaned and anlayzed it Created a Channel Economics Model to support metrics for channels and customer segments	Analytics measured profitability of various sub-segments in B2C and B2B segments	Iterate on calibration and improvement	
Sales Pipeline Improvement	Sales data not organized in a system, but scattered in multiple excel spreadsheets Lack of consolidated view of sales opportunities for B2B contracts Leveraged domestic and international Corporate Value database into Sales Data mart for analytics	Created a dashabord of Sales Pipeline opportunities by value and probabilty Estimated value of new Sales contracts	Trained Sales teams on using pipeline dashboards and analytics Iterate on getting data into the systems and on the dashboards to the Field Sales	Significant improvements in Sales closure and revenue lift (15% increase in 2 years)
Sales Force Compensation	Mapping of Sales person to territory and to Sales volumes not in place	Created dashboard and detailed reports of Sales force performance	Multiple workshops and meetings with Sales teams to familiarize with the new compensation system Iterate and improve on the dashboards and compensation system to deliver most value	More engaged and motivated sales force team
	Performance based incentives computations not in place We introduced Sales performance and compensation data into the Sales Data Mart	Incorporated Predictive Modeling and What if Scenario Modeling Developed a working model of a new Sales compensation system		Lead to 15% revenue performance improvement in 2 years
Sales Force Structure	Mapping of Sales person to territory and to Sales volumes not in place	Created models to measure Sales Force performance by territory , by level	Run models to calibrate optimal sales structure to drive best results	Balanced sales force structure and resource mapping to opportunities
	Data on Sales force drivers not captured and mapped onto performance Captured and mapped Sales and drivers data	Part of the system was to identify the mismatch of resources to drivers to sales opportunities	Iterate	Lead to 15% revenue performance improvement in 2 years
B2B Contract Modeling	All contracts data was stored in separate sales contract system Data not integrated with rest of Sales and airline systems	Created models to run an integrated view of b2b contract performance and highlight drivers Identified driver movements to increase sales performance	Run contract models pre sales and for sales performance reviews Run iteratively to improve models and usage within Sales team	Much improved retention, compliance and performance from B2B channel
	Led to disjointed understanding of client, TMC and Sales Force performance	Incorporated levers from across commercial department, not just from Sales team	Start small , but eventually include all existing and new contracts under this analytics	2% lift in revenues
Cost of Sale Reduction	Data completely fragmented. Existing in various formats in different excel spreadsheets along entire sales team No methodologies in place to allocate most costs acorss sales and marketing	Created fully allocated models that take cost of each driver in generating the sales Cost data included Sales, Promotions, Marketing cost - 360 view of costs	Run profit margins models across various channels, POS of the sales force Review with teams, iterate and improve the models	Was able to reduce cost of sale by 10% while increasing revenues by 15% over 2 years
Bottom Line Impact of Advanced Analytics Project - Increase Revenues by 15% over 2 years, COS reduced 10%				

Figure 33: Advanced Sales analytics - use case at a global airline

12.4 MULTIDIMENSIONAL UNCONSTRAINED PROFIT OPTIMIZATION

We discuss concepts of multidimensional unconstrained demand, a basis for driving cross functional commercial optimization in the advanced analytics described in this book.

Demand is generated by sales teams across POS, channels, and segments for various routes. This characteristic of demand makes it multidimensional and we start by recognizing it as that. The next step is to quantify this demand across microsegments of this multidimensional space.

Microsegments are spaces across dimensions spanning weeks and even months where customer behavior (response to drivers) is carefully understood in granularity. The purpose of understanding demand in microsegments is to be able to quantify what drives it and take decisions that increase profits.

Multidimensional demand is not constrained by supply (inventory). It is naturally developing over time as departures approach. By focusing on the flight dimension and in a bid to maximize revenue on flight departures, today's RM systems are constraining demand. Advanced analytics systems transcend this.

Demand is seen in the form of bookings which are generating revenues at a cost. The commercial profit function is sum of total revenues minus the cost of generating those bookings and is shown in the formula below:

Commercial Profit Margins = Revenues – Cost of Sales, Marketing
and Distribution

Summed over bookings in a microsegment of dimensions.

Profits are being driven daily by the bookings in the multidimensional space. Today's RM systems are focused on revenues and not profits as described above. Profits are not just an annual accounting exercise undertaken by the CFO. Airline commercial departments need to be consciously driving profits up across the multidimensional space each day. Advanced analytics systems focused on enterprise profits are the first systems that deliver to this specific needs of commercial leadership.

Advanced analytics would be running AI based forecasting algorithms on Big Data across the multidimensional space forecasting *demand and profits*. This forms the basic predictive analytics framework for most of the commercial actions. There are two components in this framework – data and models. Advanced analytics takes both components to significantly new levels and ensures enterprise wide alignment in the process.

The forecasting models will draw on data from across the commercial functions and model the drivers of demand from across functions as well. Pricing, Promotions, Distribution and Product enhancing drivers that push and pull demand will be modeled together for the first time in deriving enterprise level actions. This is the distinguishing characteristic of advanced enterprise analytics. Every lever will be modeled as a driver of enterprise results. The modeling is complete, using comprehensive enterprise data each and every time. These models are completely different from existing RM, sales, marketing and NP models which focus on departmental metrics and drivers.

Advanced analytics optimization models are predictive and prescriptive models. They are able to identify changes in conditions dynamically and using predictive analytics, translate those changes into impacts on profits in the future. This is also an important differentiating feature of advanced analytics from existing departmental systems like the RM and Sales systems, which cannot be early warning systems.

12.5   COLLECTION OF CHAPTER TAKEAWAYS

Below is a collection of all the takeaways from each chapter. This is a handy and important collection of thoughts. It will guide the CEO and the management team in thinking about advanced analytics.

Chapter 2

- Profitability of the airline industry is the lowest compared to most other industries.
- The vast majority of airlines do not have consistent profits across business cycles.
- Analytics innovation has not taken place in the airline industry as it has in other leading industries.
- Revenue management analytics has not progressed beyond its original and limited (in today's Big Data environment) paradigms of forecasting and optimization.
- Advanced analytics must be adopted by the airline industry to make it more profitable over the next few decades and restore competitiveness with other industries in turning profits.
- The CEO is the main executive who should "get this" and exhort her leaders to adopt and deliver advanced analytics. She should drive the governance of advanced analytics deployment and be on top of the review of results
- Competing airlines range from stage 1 to stage 5 in using analytics. Those in stage 5 would have a significant competitive advantage leading to increased profitable market share. They are practicing descriptive, prescriptive and predictive analytics.
- Advanced analytics uses cases of RM and Sales analytics at client airlines reveals the scope of improvements can range from 5% to 15% revenue improvements.

Chapter 3

- Analytics in airlines today is very centered on the revenue management department. Historically RM has been the main department with full access to all the critical information about flight demand and revenues, which are stored in RM systems.
- The core design and architecture of RM systems has not changed much since the advent of early systems nearly thirty years back. They focus on historical bookings and the characteristics of the bookings to forecast future demand and revenues.
- RM systems were introduced in the 1980s to serve a strategic need to bring competitive advantage using cutting-edge pricing and marketing analytics. But since then, RM has become increasingly tactical in its focus and has lost the strategic edge of dynamic pricing.
- RM economics is based on constrained supply and demand. This results in a systematic bias in forecasting and optimization leading to loss of revenue.
- RM systems are based on inventory control of Fare classes. This system may be in place due to the current GDS distribution systems, but bottom line is that it does not allow for true dynamic pricing. This results in loss of revenue.
- Demand forecasting is single or two dimensional at best, focusing on routes and flights as one dimension and fare class as another dimension. They cannot forecast various other dimensions such as POS, channels, customer segments.
- RM systems are transactional and focus on the best possible yield (or revenue) the system can deliver given capacity and demand. They do not factor in the life time value of customers when deciding on optimal value to charge.
- Today's RM systems have evolved from yield to revenue focus, but have not yet graduated toward margin and value focus. This results in

suboptimal delivery of the main metrics of the commercial department⊠ the highest possible commercial margins.

- Multidimensional unconstrained demand forecasting and optimization using advanced analytics is the next level of enterprise RM.

Chapter 4

- Big Data is not just about volume, variety, and velocity of new data. It is about both new data and complexity added to existing data with new states reached.
- Big Data is both structured data coming from conventional channels and unstructured data coming from new channels
- A significant amount of structured Big Data is residing in Excel spread-sheets across the commercial functions in airlines today. The Excel sheets also have a vast amount of business rules built into manipulating the data to feed models that are used for decision-making.
- Unlocking this Big Data in the Excel sheets and moving it into the enterprise realm with the right governance creates a significant opportunity for airlines to improve the quality and consistency of decision-making.
- Big Data has many applications within airlines to deliver significant value and ROI. Some of the main ones include product and service improvement, promotions that work, dynamic pricing that maximizes revenues, customer segmentation that increases loyalty and CLV, and operational effectiveness that drives down costs by an order of magnitude.
- Using Big Data effectively with modern predictive analytics to forecast and recommend optimal decisions is the key to advanced analytics in airlines. Doing this effectively can have a significant impact on airline profits.
- It is critical to support the scope and effort to feed advanced analytics daily. This is the daily hard work needed to provide enterprise insights to enterprise processes for optimization. Governance is critical in running the daily enterprise advanced analytics and for providing the key ingredient – Big Data.

Chapter 5

- Airlines that are able to have superior coordination across RM, sales, NP, and marketing are able to drive higher per-unit revenue of loads and yield simultaneously.
- Lack of coordination is caused by three main factors: (1) lack of focus on a single metric across the departments, (2) lack of an integrated enterprise analytics system across the departments, and (3) lack of an integrated dashboard system across the departments.
- The lack of alignment between sales and RM is caused because sales focuses on forward sales while RM focuses on flown revenue. Sales metrics are distributed and divided across POS and channels, while RM targets are distributed across flights and routes, causing the gaps in the metrics.
- ERP systems cut across departmental processes in the 1990s and helped in transactional coordination. What is needed in airlines today is a similarly integrated analytics system for decision coordination and optimization.
- The entire commercial department should be looking at the same dashboards that communicate focused common metrics in a consistent way. They all take away the same "single version of the *insights*."

Chapter 6

- Google Analytics is a great place to start understanding how modern enterprise predictive analytics should work. It works without significant IT effort to gather all the data. The enterprise analytics stack is a product tailored to deliver advanced analytics across all commercial functions and should be as easy to implement and use as Google Analytics.
- Enterprise-level predictive analytics for the airline commercial function brings together the data, modeling, and insights across the key departments of sales, RM, network planning, and marketing. In today's world, these functions source their own data, build their own models, and of

course derive their own insights, mostly within the stovepipes of their functions, not connected with the other functions.

- Delivering enterprise predictive analytics requires significant work to bring the data, modeling, and user applications together. These three ingredients can be represented as a stack of technologies bringing together the analytics.

- The Predictive Analytics stack comprises 3 main layers of the stack – data integration layers which source regular and Big Data into the databases, an all- important data models layer which integrates the data and massages it to suit all types of enterprise models and finally the models layer which drives the enterprise insights.

- Business leaders can commission vendors or the IT departments in delivering the predictive analytics stack to the commercial department.

- The CEO and CCO should use a playbook (summary in the appendix) to implement an advanced analytics culture and deliver breakthrough results. A critical part of the playbook is a build vs buy decision on the best way to get the analytics in place. Looking at past success of industry products like RM and ERP systems and the past failures of home-made systems like BI systems, we recommend that advanced analytics should be procured and not built ground up.

- A focus on business analysts is more important than building up on data scientists and statisticians. Results orientation of analyses is more important than the ability to understand the arcane math behind the models. This is being overlooked at a majority of commercial and IT departments of many airlines.

Chapter 7

- Execution takes place in microsegments of dynamic competition while strategy takes place in more static environments. This is a key reason why there is usually a gap at most airlines between expected and actual results.

- Today's state of analytics does not allow for most of the commercial functions to be able to track this gap in real time and correct course.
- To address this would be a top priority for airline managements worldwide. It would require a business process reengineering of the commercial function. Specifically, the reengineering should be focused on the following aspects:
  - o Development of enterprise analytics capabilities in the commercial function
  - o Development of enterprise insights to guide the strategy and execution process
  - o Institution of governance for enterprise analytics
- Advanced Enterprise Analytics is a paradigm-shifting capability that can enable airlines to execute better and deliver better results. Predictive and prescriptive analytics based on Big Data provide the best possible navigation in the dynamic and volatile execution environment.
- Real-time insights generated from the advanced analytics capability are communicated down and up the hierarchy of the commercial department. This enables the whole department to be united in pursuit of the common metrics and minimize execution risk.
- The C-Suite and the new function of Chief Analytics Officer work in concert and lead the governance process. They implement the advanced analytics capability and they use insights top down in all meeting forums to guide the teams to superior execution.

Chapter 8

- Most airlines are using outdated dashboards that are primarily backward-looking reports. These dashboards are not reliable to provide consistent insights across the commercial departments to drive the optimal decisions.
- The futuristic dashboards of Analytics 3.0 are powered by predictive analytics piping insights to management across the commercial departments.

Analytical predictive models working on real-time Big Data are generating forward-looking insights in these futuristic dashboards.

- These dashboards follow the best design principles: they are intuitive, motivating, insightful, and certified. They aggregate and drill down among all the dimensions along which the key metrics and drivers need to be understood by management for decisions.

- The futuristic dashboards are used by all managers across the commercial departments for their decisions. It is the one source of the truth, delivering the same insights to all without need for interpretation. These dashboards are an integral part of the advanced analytics system of the airline.

- Commercial dashboards show results and drivers in the same look and feel across all dimensions and at all levels of the organization. This helps the commercial team to be always consistent in presenting and interpreting data. Results are presented with profit metrics and drivers. Aligning the whole commercial department on the same metric is critical for alignment.

- Smart graphs are a critical part of modern analytics dashboards. They are powered by real time predictive analytics and allow for drill downs, scenario modeling and dynamic what-if analytics. They should eventually eliminate excel spreadsheets which are at present the main analytics tools, albeit with limited data and modeling that is non-standard.

- Using these dashboards, managers can take decisions by literally being on the same page at any end of the process. Standard predictive models are run and presented with the same insights to all users, ensuring alignment. This single innovation in dashboard science is more important than any other in driving better commercial decisions.

Chapter 9

- RM systems are operational systems more so than analytical systems. Hence they are not designed or wired to help the company with all types of analytics needed across the enterprise. Their data repositories are not designed to help answer analytical questions around sales channels, promotions, or specific customer segments.

- RM systems have not been reinvented to make them drivers of Big Data analytics across the enterprise. Instead they have superficially changed to work with Big Data, without changing any of their core mathematical models.
- Using Multidimensional Predictive Analytics, RM systems can fundamentally improve forecasting all around. They deliver a forecasting system for the entire commercial department including RM, sales, marketing, and network planning. A system that forecasts bookings, revenues, and profits, not just bookings. A system that can provide what-if forecasting analytics with changing drivers
- This RM system can forecast bookings and cancellations more accurately on all dimensions, which sets up the platform for better Overbooking and Revenue Integrity.
- Advanced analytics based RM systems can identify dynamic pricing opportunities in the multidimensional space. Pricing inversions can be spotted and highlighted as they are forming, saving significant revenue dilution.
- Advanced analytics based RM systems can dynamically evaluate and optimize tradeoffs in connecting vs local traffic and online vs interline traffic.
- The above notwithstanding, a complete advanced analytics based RM system highlights every opportunity through dynamic dashboards to the entire commercial department. This takes RM enterprise wide from being a functional process.

Chapter 10

- Sales teams are distributed across the airlines' footprint of sales and depend on headquarters based reports to help them execute. For the most part they receive standard backward looking reports on performance and forward looking bookings reports. Any analytics is done in excel environment. Given this environment of distributed teams, lack of strong analytics systems and basic reports to work from, modern sales teams need a significant boost of analytics to outperform competition.

- While RM has their own system for operational analytics, Sales teams do not have any such system. Advanced analytics systems deliver a significant advantage to this crucial department which along with RM is tasked with delivering the commercial revenue.

- Advanced analytics can deliver a significant advantage by automating the modeling and decision support in several key sales processes such as channel management, agency management, sales force management and client management.

- Advanced analytics provides significant improvement in customer loyalty through predictive analytics techniques that take customer lifetime value creation as central to customer decisions. This enables the entire commercial organization to make decisions that always increase the lifetime value of the customer base.

- These analytics can show the risks that are emerging in the future space and the actions needed to deliver optimal performance. Delivered through motivating and insightful gamification-based screens, such a system can elevate average teams to super performing sales teams.

Chapter 11

- Hotel industry advanced analytics is similar to that in the airline industry. Using advanced analytics, the hotel industry can address some shortcomings of RM-driven analytics so far.

- RM in the hotel industry should move beyond room-based revenues. They must include a complete revenue perspective that brings food-and-banqueting revenues and meetings-and-conventions revenues into the optimization paradigm along with room revenues.

- The hotel industry should further understand the changing dynamic of distribution costs, which are threatening their margins. Traditional TMC and GDS channels are decreasing, while OTA and Brand.com are increasing their share. This is not always the best result or the best strategy. Yields, costs, and margins should be fully factored in, and optimizing commercial margins (GOP) rather than revenues is the way forward.

- Travel management companies are critical intermediaries in the airline and travel market. They play an important role for profitability of airlines and hotels as they control clients who are the bread and butter of the corporate travel segment.

- Advanced analytics can bring together the different departments of the TMC like sales, supplier management, operations, client management, and HR. Today most of these analytics are being executed in silos as in the airline and hotel industries. It is imperative for the CEOs of this industry to develop advanced analytics systems to optimize profit margins and not just pass along the burden to the source of inventory they help optimize.

12.6 Index

12.7   References

i   Erik Brynjolfsson on Big Data: A revolution in decision-making improves productivity. http://mitsloanexperts.mit.edu/erik-brynjolfsson-on-big-data-a-revolution-in-decision-making-improves-productivity/

ii   McKinsey: Big Data – The next frontier for innovation, competition and productivity.   http://www.mckinsey.com/business-functions/business-technology/our-insights/big-data-the-next-frontier-for-innovation

iii   Thomas H Davenport: At the Big Data Crossroads: turning toward a smarter travel experience – Amadeus research report 2013

iv   Thomas H Davenport and Jeanne G Harris, Analytics at Work: Smarter Decisions, Better Results

v   Ben Vinod: Evolution of yield management in travel, Journal of Pricing and Revenue Management, July 2016

vi   Cynthia Barnhart and Barry Smith, "Quantitative Problem Solving Methods in the Airline Industry", 2012

vii   A O Lee: Airline reservations forecasting probabilistic and statistical models of the booking process, MIT 1990

viii   L. R. Weatherford and P. P. Belobaba, "Revenue impacts of fare input and demand forecast accuracy in airline yield management," Journal of the Operational Research Society, vol. 53, no. 8

ix   Ben Vinod: Evolution of yield management in travel, Journal of Pricing and Revenue Management, July 2016

x   http://www.mckinsey.com/insights/business_technology/big_data_the_next_frontier_for_innovation

xi   Colin Ellis: "Why half your projects will fail this year and what you can do about it", CIO, August 2015

xii   Ram Charan and Larry Bossidy, Execution: The discipline of getting things done

xiii   Karl Isler and Elton D'Souza, "GDS Capabilities, OD control and dynamic pricing", Journey of Revenue and Pricing Management, 2009

xiv   Aswath Damodaran: US companies Profit Margins 2015(net, operating and Ebitda), www.damodaran.com, www.nyu.edu